The rights of the sovereignty vindicated. With particular reference to political doctrines of the Edinburgh review, and of other periodical publications

John Pern Tinney

Nabu Public Domain Reprints:

You are holding a reproduction of an original work published before 1923 that is in the public domain in the United States of America, and possibly other countries. You may freely copy and distribute this work as no entity (individual or corporate) has a copyright on the body of the work. This book may contain prior copyright references, and library stamps (as most of these works were scanned from library copies). These have been scanned and retained as part of the historical artifact.

This book may have occasional imperfections such as missing or blurred pages, poor pictures, errant marks, etc. that were either part of the original artifact, or were introduced by the scanning process. We believe this work is culturally important, and despite the imperfections, have elected to bring it back into print as part of our continuing commitment to the preservation of printed works worldwide. We appreciate your understanding of the imperfections in the preservation process, and hope you enjoy this valuable book.

Digitized for Microsoft Corporation
by the Internet Archive in 2007.
From University of California Libraries.
May be used for non-commercial, personal, rese
or educational purposes, or any fair use.
May not be indexed in a commercial service

THE
RIGHTS
OF THE
SOVEREIGNTY
VINDICATED.

WITH PARTICULAR REFERENCE TO POLITICAL DOCTRINES
OF THE EDINBURGH REVIEW, AND OF OTHER
PERIODICAL PUBLICATIONS.

BY JOHN PERN TINNEY, Esq.

―――――

—ὥτε Ζεὺς κυδος ἐδωκεν.

LONDON:

PRINTED BY AND FOR C. AND R. BALDWIN, NEW BRIDGE-STREET;
AND FOR BRODIE AND CO. SALISBURY.

1809.

U.

ADVERTISEMENT.

This Publication was begun in November, but was suspended on account of Mr. Wharton's intended work, of which the Author was apprized.

That work has appeared, and been very favourably received. As the Author's plan was somewhat more extensive than Mr. Wharton's, he has ventured to proceed in the execution of it. Recent events have shewn the infinite importance of the subject. It will be a sufficient reward to him, if, by his feebler efforts, he may contribute to that triumph of reason which can only be effected, at this alarming crisis, by the zealous and active co-operation of all the friends of our antient institutions.

U

TO THE

REV. WILLIAM COXE, A.M.

ARCHDEACON OF WILTS, CANON RESIDENTIARY OF SALISBURY, &c. &c.

—

In the following pages I have endeavoured, as well by some discussion of the fatal influence of certain growing opinions, as by reference to past events recorded in authentic history, to defend the institutions of society, against a sect of reformers, still militant among us.

I am anxious to obtain the approbation of those, whose superior judgment and extensive knowledge, entitle them to decide the important controversy; and chiefly of one whom posterity will regard as a distinguished promoter of sound philosophy and liberal science, and consult as the most eminent historian of the present age.

In the hope of that approbation, permit me, Sir, to lay the following pages before you; and in acknowledgement of that friendship, by which I have been gratified and improved, to subscribe myself,

Your most obliged and faithful servant,

J. P. TINNEY.

U

TABLE OF THE CONTENTS.

PART THE FIRST.

Of the Affairs of Spain.

INFLUENCE of Public Opinion	1
Political Doctrines of the Edinburgh Review	5
Difficulties and Prospect of the Patriots of Spain	7
The Statement of the Reviewers upon that Subject	15
Refutation of their Statement of Facts	18
The Nature of the Spanish Monarchy	20
The Proceedings in Spain similar to those in England in 1688	21
The Present State of the Parties in Spain	31
Examination of the Anti-monarchical Doctrine of the Reviewers	33
Opinions tending to establish the Aristocracy of Talents	38

PART THE SECOND.

Of the Aristocracy of Talents.

Origin and Progress of Political Opinion	43
The Elder Philosophers, *practical*	45
Origin of Society	47
The Foundation of the Republic of Letters	52
Their earliest Proceedings to weaken Personal Respect towards Superiors	53
Their Impious and Immoral Doctrines	55
Their *Speculative* Doctrine of the Rights of Man	56
Their Resemblance to the Catilinarian Conspiracy	59
The Foundation of the Aristocracy of Talents and Origin of Jacobinism	60
Its Necessary Effects	63
Louis XVI. guided by that Aristocracy—his Character and Fate	64
Short Triumph of the Philosophers	68
The Unprecedented Principles of the Revolution	69
Its Tendency to Military Despotism	74
Rise, Character, and Government of Bonaparte	78
Favoured by the Aristocracy of Talents	95
The Literature of England, and its System of Education	97
Application to the Proceedings in Spain	105

PART THE THIRD.

Of the British Constitution.

Statute of Merton	107
Magna Charta	110
Antiquity of the Constitution	111
The Privileges of the Subject	118
Prerogative of the Crown	119
Influence of the Crown	120
In Parliament	121
Privileges and Uses of the Peerage	135
The Right of Universal Suffrage and Elective Franchise	143
The House of Commons	149
Case of the Duke of York	151
Instances of the Predominating Influence of Popular Opinion on our Government	155
Apostacy of the Authors of the Political Register and Edinburgh Review	157

PART THE FOURTH.

Of the Present Danger of the Constitution.

State of the Public Mind in 1792	160
Pacific System of Mr. Pitt	161
Reviewers' Statement of the War of 1793	163
Origin and Nature of that War	164
Unbounded Ambition of France	179
Our Immediate Duties	184
Censures of Government and the Established Authorities by Disaffected Writers	186
Their Attacks of the Higher Orders	187
Their own Partisans exempted	193
Their Insiduous Object	197
Public Thanks to Mr. Wardle and his Minority	198
Interference of the People with their representatives, unconstitutional	199
Revolutions unfavourable to Intellectual Improvement, historically proved	202
Present Freedom and Prosperity of Britain	205
To be preserved by Resistance to the Advocates of Jacobinical Reform	208

THE RIGHTS OF THE SOVEREIGNTY.

PART THE FIRST.

THE History of the World will prove, that, although the opinions of mankind may be much influenced by the nature of political institutions, and by circumstances which are independent of human policy, yet the stability, and in most cases, the origin of all such institutions, depend upon the course of popular sentiment, which is often powerfully impelled and directed, by those who claim and exercise a sort of despotic sway in matters of literature and philosophy. The proudest domination ever exercised over the human mind, and over the governments of nations, was raised on the foundation of opinion. Its authority was never limited, nor did its grandeur fade, 'till the spirit of rational inquiry raised in the seminaries of the learned, was from thence diffused through the various departments of society. Then the support of opinion was gradually withdrawn from the Roman hierarchy; and after a thousand years, during which it had held kings in bondage, and disposed of empires with fearless prodigality, it fell before the assault of an obscure

Augustin monk. In our own day, the most antient and the proudest monarchy in Europe, which was rooted in the ordinances of distant generations, and had long been matured in power and splendour by the provisions of a sound and vigorous policy, has fallen without resistance, when it no longer rested upon the basis of opinion. The domestic difficulties which preceded the uproar of the French revolution, might have happened at any preceding period without endangering the state: all parties will agree, that at last it proceeded from a great change in the opinions of the people; and " it is difficult to deny that the " philosophers were instrumental in bringing about " that change; that they had attracted the public " attention to the abuses of government, and " spread very widely among the people the senti-" ments of their grievances and their rights."[*]

The philosophers had attracted the public attention to every thing in the government which wore the aspect of abuse; deceived by their instruction and seduced by their example, the people were irritated by imaginary grievances, and flattered by fictitious rights. Their influence was not limited to France, but had extended over the whole Continent of Europe, as widely as the philosophy which they promulged, and the literature over which they presided. In all countries, the people instructed by those philosophers, considered the war which was occasioned by the excesses of the revolution, as an unnatural struggle between the supporters of antient despotism and the asserters of the newly discovered rights of man. The most formidable enemies of the allied

[*] 1. Edin. Rev. 8. The article is a review of Mounier's "Traité de l'Influence attribuée aux Philosophes," and is well worthy of perusal.

sovereigns were their own disaffected subjects. The disastrous progress and fatal termination of that contest, too plainly shewed what an awful change of popular opinion had been effected in every country; and how vain are the efforts of princes unaided by such opinion.

Convinced not only that the manners of society are eminently influenced by its literature, but also that all political institutions must yield to a similar operation, no one who venerates the constitution of this country, and the loyalty and morality of its people, can observe with indifference the doctrines continually advanced by certain writers, who, from whatever cause, possess a powerful influence over the public mind. In other states popular opinion does not operate with a constant and equal effect upon the administration of affairs. Government being less intimately connected with its subjects, and the people having no civil function to discharge, the state proceeds in its ordinary course without that controul, and the public voice is seldom heard, but when raised with the clamour of disaffection for purposes of revolution. In England, the government is in all its proceedings, much influenced by the course of public sentiment. As at every period of its highest glory it was borne in that elevation by the favour of a generous and enthusiastic commonalty, in like manner, when deprived of that support, every measure of administration has been weak and indecisive, and ultimately, with whatever reluctance, ministers have been compelled to yield their own will and policy to the dictates of such opinion. In former periods, revolutions have ensued from a contrary determination on the part of the established powers; at present, a similar result, or at least some great national calamity might be apprehended, if the public will should become decidedly adverse to the existing government.

From this habitual and necessary conformity of government to public opinion, and from the wisdom and moderation with which that opinion has been formed, since the free exercise of our constitution was effectuated by King William, have we derived the energy which has enabled us gloriously to prevail in many arduous contests. To that cause we may attribute our present prosperity, such as our forefathers could never anticipate; and the enjoyment of domestic advantages, which nothing would so much endanger as national disunion. To that alone can we rationally look for support in our present contest, far more arduous than those of preceding ages; and for transmitting to future times the blessings enjoyed by us. Therefore, we cannot regard without alarm, a co-operation of political writers, who, like the philosophic inventors of the anarchy of the French revolution, are soliciting the public mind to mistrust and dissatisfaction; who call our attention to imputed grievances, not upon any principle of a constitutional redress, but upon a speculative foundation of injured rights; who not only censure the administrators of authority for indiscretion, incompetence, and abuses, but question its validity and object to its fundamental laws. These active and loquacious complainants have acquired no inconsiderable influence over the public mind. "They have excited a very
" general spirit of discontent, distrust, and con-
" tempt for public characters, among the more
" intelligent and resolute portion of the inferior
" ranks of society. The seeds of a revolution may
" be seen in the present aspect and temper of

" the nation, and though one looks forward to it
" with other feelings and other dispositions,"
than those who triumphantly predict it, and labour
to accomplish their own prediction; though one
trusts that those seeds are not widely disseminated,
and may yet be rooted out by those who love the
peace of their country and value its prosperity,
" yet one is not the less sensible of the hazard
" in which we are placed."*

The editors of the Edinburgh Review have lately published doctrines not hostile to that revolution which at one time they seemed to dread. From the skilfulness of their criticism, their reputation for extensive learning, the popularity of many subjects which they have selected for consideration, their fame for disinterested judgment, and the high character which they justly acquired by their earlier publications, they now enjoy an important pre-eminence over other journalists and literary reviewers. Their authority may be less extensive than they desire, or probably believe, and with the learned and well-informed, is not promoted by those extraneous political disquisitions, which they make an essential part of their work. Yet undoubtedly they have much influence upon the unlettered and the unsuspicious; upon those whose opinions must be formed upon the reasoning of others, and those who will give credit to a " high tone of patriotism and inde-
" pendence."†

They have made a particular discussion of the affairs of Spain, in the review of a sixpenny pamphlet published by Mr. Whitbread, and a state paper of Don Pedro Cevallos, compiled for the

* 10. Edin. Rev.—Review of Cobbett's Political Register.
† 10. Edin. Rev. 387.

use of the Spanish patriots. Those performances had no connection with literature or science, and might have been exempt from critical examination, without any breach of the duty of a reviewer. If worthy of such supervision, the Edinburgh reviewers had undertaken to deliver their judgment upon them, although the details must be political, yet the inquiry might have been confined to the foreign relations subsisting between the countries referred to. General declamation seems obtrusive; far less necessary was an introduction of principles upon contested points of constitutional doctrine, which convulse the passions of men, and have never yet afforded any practical advantage.

In their original advertisement, they proposed " to confine their notice to works that either " should attain or deserve a certain portion of " celebrity." The title of their publication is that of a " Critical Journal." Their plans are much affected by their newly professed fondness for " radical reform, change, and revolution." Speculations are now attached to the titles of little ephemeral tracts, the ebullitions of party spirit, which the press daily pours forth, and which, without their notice, would, like bubbles of troubled water, burst and be forgotten. And thus they make up the farrago of their work; and having announced the title of any publication, upon any subject of which they chuse to treat, " they feel it scarcely necessary to lay before " their readers any abstract of the tale unfolded " by their author, and hasten to express their " own reflections."*

In October last, having made some remarks upon the personal history and character of Don

Pedro, they proffer a series of melancholy reflections upon the prodigious difficulties to be overcome by the patriots of Spain, in their present generous warfare; and notwithstanding the great advantages which had then been gained over the armies of France, "they forebode, that it " will lead to the subjugation of the most gallant " people in the world."

Formidable indeed are those difficulties; delusive and treacherous to the gallant patriots of Spain, and to their generous allies the patriots of England, would be that counsel, which should promise an easy or speedy termination to the important warfare. The palm for which they contend is placed upon a stupendous height, and guarded by that mighty power, which, ever watchful, and ever active, as yet has never known a failure of his gigantic purposes. It is secured by all sorts of obstacles and premunitions, which may indeed be surmounted by patience of labour, by endurance of hardship and privation, by submission to all sorts of peril and necessity, and by that unyielding firmness in contempt of disaster and defeat, which none but heroes can acquire. It is only to be gained by a struggle with all manner of difficulties, by a contempt of slaughter and devastation during a long probation of calamity and fearful enterprize. But the noble achievements made by the patriotic phalanx in their unimproved condition, and the lessons of experience taught by history in many a similar conjuncture, may even yet afford us a fairer hope and a more consoling expectation.

The late failure of the British expedition, though it concluded with a victory hardly less brilliant than that obtained at Agincourt by the retreating army of Henry V. seems to have abated our hopes, and our generous interest in Spanish affairs.

We forget the flight of the usurper from Madrid, the surrender of Dupont, and the ever memorable defences of Zaragoza. We forget that, when the enemy had obtained possession of half that town, and proffered " la capitulation," the answer of its brave inhabitants was " Guerra al cuchillo." We forget that Palafox, whose name will adorn the page of history, and his brave council, resolved, " that those quarters of the city in which the " Arragonese yet maintained themselves, should " continue to be defended with the same firmness " which had hitherto been so conspicuous; should " the enemy at last prevail, the people were im- " mediately to retire by the bridge over the Ebro " into the suburbs, and having destroyed the " bridge, to defend the suburbs till they perished." We forget that the parts of the city not possessed by the enemy were gallantly defended, and that his inglorious flight " terminated the first siege of " Zaragoza; which, whether it be considered with " reference to the superiority of the means of " annoyance in possession of the enemy, to the " utter incapability of the place to resist a regular " and continued attack, to the instances of col- " lective and individual courage, to the patience " and heroism of its defenders of either sex, and " in every situation of life, can be deemed second " to none recorded in the annals of antient or " modern times:"[*] or second only to that more recent defence, which has not been equally successful, though equally heroic and exemplary.

The patriotic forces have displayed in adversity and success, that temperance and firmness, which have often secured the fruits of victory, and broken the violence of misfortune. In the day of triumph they have remembered, that the fate

[*] See Vaughan's Account of the Siege of Zaragoza.

of war is undetermined, while the enemy remains in hostile array, and have not, like vulgar minds, broken out in unmannerly exultation.

" Nescia mens hominum fati sortisque futuræ,
" Et servare modum rebus sublata secundis."

In the severer probation of defeat, they have not lost their fortitude, equanimity, and hope. They have shewn that they can bear the discipline of calamity, though they are deserving of success, brilliant as heroic virtue ever achieved. They have proved, that in their mind the spirit of liberty is associated with patience, foresight, and prudence; and whatever may be their ultimate destiny, they have already offered a brilliant example, which their posterity will long remember.

Thus associated, the spirit of liberty is unconquerable. It was that spirit of liberty which animated the barons of this nation when they exacted the great charter of our immunities, at a period when all the rest of Europe languished in unlettered and contented bondage: and by which, during seven succeeding centuries, the fabric of our free constitution has been gradually reared. That spirit, perfected by long possession, and regulated by the wisdom of the legislature, produces in our minds a generous sympathy, with whatever people struggling in the same cause shall solicit our assistance. Not that we can sympathize with the exertions of those, who, even after long servitude and oppression, shall make the name of freedom a watch-word for insurrection, and a pretence for outrage and cruelty, as contrary to our spirit of liberty, as to that moral restraint proceeding from constitutional government, without which liberty cannot subsist. Neither the ferocious multitudes, who exercised the majesty of the people in the excesses of the French revolution, nor the Negro insurgents of San Domingo, not less savage and licentious, when they broke the fetters of their subjection, could obtain from us assistance and fraternal counsel. The people of England, enthusiastic in the cause of liberty, but equally attached to government and order, will sustain with a powerful hand the efforts of any nation soliciting its co-operation against a cruel foreign usurper, preparing to enchain them with oppressive and unlawful bonds: but if that solicitation were made by insurgent rebels, or accompanied by jargon proclamations of equality and the rights of men, and by sophistical declarations of the club-house orators and preachers of the new principles of sedition, our government would never be misled by a shew of political advantage to fraternize our brave soldiery with the advocates of such a cause; nor would our loyalty induce us to approach the throne with a pledge of unlimited supplies for the furtherance of such revolution.

A great people, determined in any cause whatever, to emancipate itself from any species of tyranny, or to secure its national independence against a foreign invader, will finally succeed in its undertaking if history speak truth.

When the Athenians could no longer defend their city and their domestic gods against the overpowering force of the Persian barbarian, in the last extremity, rather than yield their liberties which they preferred to life itself, instructed by their oracle, and led by Themistocles, their great commander, they abandoned their native soil and took refuge in their ships. The fierce invader could drive them from their strong holds, possess their towns, plunder their temples, and rase their defenceless villages querable spirit of independence was too strong even for his mighty force, when his ambition was lowered by many fruitless efforts to subdue a people animated by that spirit, he, Xerxes, the great invader, fled from the despised Greeks, discomfited and disgraced. His army perished, and he alone, whose arrogance had vaunted that he would conquer Greece and enchain the sea itself, returned in a fishing bark to recite the tale of his great overthrow, which happily has reached posterity "a memorable lesson to all tyrants and a cheering example to every people."

Not less worthy of recollection are instances of the triumph of that same spirit in the records of modern history. The powers of Europe, confederated by the league of Cambray, and aided by him, whom a senseless superstition endued with more than mortal power, with military preparation, such as the world had not before witnessed, could not overcome the resistance of the little Venetian republic. The unbroken power of the Spanish monarch could not quell the spirit of independence, which placed the illustrious family of Braganza upon the throne of Portugal. The virtuous peasantry of the Helvetic mountains, in the most righteous of all causes, established their independent union in defiance of the gigantic power of the House of Austria. The Scottish nation, impelled by William Wallace, preserved its freedom against one of the mightiest of our English monarchs. Not the energy, nor the profusion, nor the deep policy of Philip the Second could avail against that hardy race, which, established under the heroic prince of Orange the republic of the United States. In later times, the people of America determined to abandon their allegiance to our imperial crown, and all the efforts of this great nation could not reduce them to their former dependence; while they retained their forests and their spirit of independence, not the utmost force of the British empire, by Lord Chatham pronounced capable of achieving any thing but impossibilities, assisted by its Indian auxiliaries, was able to subdue them. The French nation itself has afforded examples never to be overlooked. The victories of Cressy, of Poitiers, and of Azincourt, and the possession of their capital were ineffectual in older times to subject them to an English prince. After a contest, the longest which history records, marked by the greatest misfortunes, and apparently desperate in its whole continuance, the resolution of the people never to yield, at last saved the monarchy; and their virtue and vigour were rewarded with complete success. In like manner did that nation retain a chivalrous hardihood of independence after their discomfiture in the field of Pavia, where their gallant king, without the loss of honor, passed from the glory of arms to bondage in his rival's capital. The monarch retained the majesty of his title, and the people their undaunted resolution to maintain it. He was at last rewarded with recovering his freedom, and his royalty unimpaired; and they, at no distant period, with victories over the imperial house which blotted out the stain, if any stain there were, of their defeat at Pavia. The same nation has given a recent instance of the effect of that same spirit; (lamentable indeed for the crime and the delusion which occasioned it!) The democracy of France having provoked the continental war, was in contest with powerful states on every side justly jealous of their first advances towards that greatness which now eclipses the greatness of all other potentates. The angry multitude were taught that their independence was in danger; they never despaired, although they were without a general, without an army, and without finance. Their enemy formed the grandest alliance which Europe could afford, supplicated, encouraged, and assisted by all the rank, power, property, and consideration of the ancient monarchy. The energy of the people saved the French republic. Although we never sympathized with that success, yet it affords the last living proof that a great nation determined to be independent of foreign rule must accomplish its purpose.

Let us not be taught that the changes effected by the greatness and example of France have so powerful a controul over moral nature and human affairs, that now the enthusiasm of a bold and hardy nation can be successful only in an unrighteous cause. Let us trust that the spirit of liberty so nobly displayed in the proceedings of the Spanish nation, though it did not shew itself in outrage, tumult, and massacre, though it was accompanied by a faithful adherence to the principles of order and justice, and though it was associated with a loyal attachment to a lawful and injured sovereign, may prevail, as the same spirit in so many former instances has prevailed, against the machinations and force of a cruel, treacherous, and hated usurpation.

Though the events of the last campaign did not answer the hopes which were inspired by its glorious commencement, and the capital of Spain is now in the possession of France, yet the people of England are too much dispirited by recent calamities. Immediate triumph could not be rationally expected. Numberless as are the Spanish patriots, and undaunted as they have shewn themselves in the spirit which animates them, it was impossible that in a short period they could consolidate an instructed and disciplined force sufficient to contend with the concentrated armies dispatched against them by military France. Our hope ought to be prospective. We may be sure that the usurper will gain many victories, but we must trust that his power will not extend far beyond the limits of the conquered field. If the Spanish population remain hostile to his interests, (and what event should make us mistrust their perseverance?) an opposing army must inevitably grow, which shall at last tear the laurels from the victor's brow, and drive away the hosts of his slaves, the instruments of his boundless ambition.

The success of his usurpation would, undoubtedly, be a greater calamity than any other which could happen to the continent of Europe. It would more firmly rivet the chains which an unexampled despotism has fastened upon the vanquished nations, and would be the proudest military triumph in the annals of the modern conqueror. It would extinguish the last apparent hope of loyalty and ancient honor, and might fix upon an unassailable rock the throne of the champion of revolutions.

In the early jacobinism of France, there was nothing national or particular. Its leaders in their first success looked far beyond the overthrow of the greatest monarchy in Europe, and valued that, their first achievement, but as the means of extending the conflagration of revolution to the four corners of the world. For the furtherance of that object they were reconciled to all the misery by which society was desolated and afflicted, and never felt " the compunctious visitings of nature" for their abundant share in producing it. Whoever has adopted the notions of their morality, and will assent to the purchase of probable advantage at the expence of certain evil, (which assent I conceive to be a fundamental abomination of the new philosophy;) that person will estimate the most aweful events of the moral world as the gradations of an arithmetical process; and will consider the account not unfavorable if the balance calculated according to the modern valuation of the natural rights of men, and the comparative worthlessness of all the domestic duties, be on the side of the natural rights. The Edinburgh reviewers can turn their view from the calamities to result from a failure of the cause of the patriots in Spain, and be comforted " by contemplating the effects of the " struggle upon civil liberty, and *that* the rather " because a part of those good consequences are " likely to ensue from the glorious efforts already " made, although it should terminate unsuccess- " fully."

They tell us that " the resistance to France has " been entirely begun and carried on by the peo- " ple in Spain. Their kings betrayed them, fled, " and rushed, with the whole of their base cour- " tiers, into the arms of the enemy. Their nobles " followed, and it is painful to reflect, that some " of the most distinguished of this body, after at- " tending Ferdinand to Bayonne, returned in the " train of Joseph, and only quitted his service when " the universal insurrection of the common peo- " ple drove him from his usurped throne. The " people, then, and, of the people, the middle, " and, above all, the lower orders have alone the " merit of raising this glorious opposition to the " common enemy of national independence. Those " who had so little of what is commonly termed " interest in the country, those who had no stake " in the community (to speak the technical lan- " guage of the aristocracy,) the persons of no con- " sideration in the state, they who could not " pledge their fortunes, having only lives and li- " berties to lose; the bulk, the mass of the people, " nay the very odious, many headed beast, the " multitude, the mob itself, alone uncalled, un- " aided by the higher classes, and in direct oppo-

"sition to them, as well as to the enemy whom
" they so vilely joined, raised up the standard of in-
" surrection, bore it through massacre and through
" victory, until it chased the usurper away, and
" waved over his deserted courts. Happen what
" will in the sequel, here is a grand and perma-
" nent success, a lesson to all governments, a
" warning to all oligarchies, a cheering example to
" every people. Not a name of note in Spain was
" to be seen in the records of the patriotic pro-
" ceedings, until the cause began to flourish; and
" then the high orders came round for their share
" in the success. The Spaniards then owe their
" victory, whether it unhappily stops short at its
" present point, or ends in the expulsion of the
" invaders, wholly to the efforts of the people.

" Suppose for a moment that they succeed;
" that France gives way before she tries the issue
" of the impending contest; or is finally defeated,
" and Spain freed: will the gallant people, after
" performing such wonders, quietly open the doors
" of the Escurial to the same herd of crowned or
" titled intriguers, who first, by misruling the mo-
" narchy, and then by deserting it in that utmost
" need into which their misrule had brought it,
" had rendered necessary all the effusion of blood,
" and had almost rendered it vain? Having shed
" their best blood in rescuing their house from a
" banditti admitted by the cowardice or treachery
" of the watchmen, will the Spaniards be such
" fools as to restore those poltroons and traitors to
" their former posts, and renew a confidence so
" universally abused? No man can hesitate one
" instant in saying, that this thing neither ought
" to be, nor will be. Common justice demands
" such a change of government as will give the
" people who have saved the state, who have re-
" conquered it, a fair salvage, a large share in its

" future management. Common sense requires
" an alteration in the political constitution of the
" monarchy, sufficiently radical to guard it against
" a recurrence of the late crisis. And if all con-
" sideration of justice and of prudence were out
" of the question, the Spanish court may be as-
" sured of this, that the feelings of our common
" nature, the universal sentiments of right and
" of pride which must prevail among a people ca-
" pable of such gallant deeds, will prevent the re-
" petition of the former abuses, and carry reform,
" change, revolution (we dread not the use of this
" word, so popular in England before the late reign
" of terror), salutary, just, and necessary revolu-
" tion, over all the departments of the state.

" Such, we may be assured, will be the immedi-
" ate consequence of the Spaniards ultimately tri-
" umphing over their enemies, and restoring the
" peninsula to independence. Whether Ferdi-
" nand or Charles be the monarch, we care not;
" or whether a new stock be brought from Ger-
" many for a breed. That they should have a king
" every one must admit, who believes that an he-
" reditary monarch, well fettered by the constitu-
" tion, is the best guardian of civil liberty. But
" who the monarch is, must be a matter of little
" moment, provided he is sufficiently controuled
" in the exercise of his delegated and responsible
" trust. And whatever may be the form of the
" checks imposed upon him, we shall be satisfied,
" provided the basis of a free constitution is laid
" deep and steady in a popular representation.
" Many years must elapse before this can be cor-
" rupted, and betray the people to the crown; for
" the general sentiments of liberty, of contempt
" for bad rulers, of resistance to all enemies, fo-
" reign and domestic, the universal feeling of their

" own powers from the recollection of their great
" actions, will long remain among the Spanish
" People, and shake to atoms every court intrigue
" hostile to their rights."

In these passages there is much speculative doctrine, and some historical narration.

The speculative doctrine is the same that flowed from our disaffected clubs in England, and from that great vortex of revolutionary principles, the club, which exercised the powers of Government in France, after the final overthrow of royalty. My immediate purpose will be to shew, that the matter of the historical narration is altogether unfounded in fact, and grossly libellous of the character of the Spanish nation.

And first I presume to inquire, whether any proclamation or proceeding of any of the assemblies which have most wisely conducted the grand movement of the Spanish nation, was made upon the principle which melancholy experience has rendered too familiar to us, of " reform, change, " and revolution." None such is quoted by the Edinburgh Reviewers; if any such have taken place, the English nation has been much deceived.

If that transaction was a great simultaneous effort of every order and degree of the universal Spanish nation, in opposition to an unprincipled usurper, and his intriguing courtiers, made in the name and in the cause of him whom they considered their lawful sovereign, the narration of the reviewers seems to bear little resemblance to the authentic fact. It is a distorted portraiture highly colored and strongly delineated, but not designed from any existing features of the character displayed by that magnanimous confederacy. It is a shapeless and unnatural monster, such as the world never saw, but in the triumph of traitors at the downfal of the French monarchy, suited to the abominable idolatry of that triumph, but little calculated to obtain the homage of the British public.

In a plain concise relation of the remote causes and the circumstances of that transaction, there is nothing to gratify the wishes of those among us who pant for revolution, but much to console the drooping spirits of such as lament the subjugation of the continent, and of such as retain unimpaired their love and admiration of that order and liberty which the constitution of this country has perfectly combined. It is an interesting spectacle, at this period of great calamity, to behold a powerful nation, which were among the first to bend in fatal homage to the terrific supremacy of France, and endeavoured to conciliate that insatiate power by yielding their richest colonies to its sovereignty, by sustaining its prodigality with their treasure, by recruiting its armies from their population, by endeavouring to maintain its maritime strength by their navy, by a patient submission to the ingratitude, insult, and indignity, which, in return for such services, were every hour accumulated to prepare their minds for absolute subjection; to behold that nation, like the lion when he turns upon his hunters, roused to destructive vengeance. They were the first to check the tyrant in his course; and while their manly purpose, for the first time, convulsed his mind with just alarm, they afforded the first great national proof that the new principles of anarchy are not universal, and that a people may be terrible to a usurper, without disloyalty or faction.

To such as admire the British constitution, and can applaud those firm and moderate measures, which led to its completion in 1688, there appears in that spectacle a similarity of circumstance and design, which is alike honorable to this country, which gave the great example, and to that which has wisely followed it. The principle of both those events is the same; not that of "reform, " radical change, and revolution;" unless the amendment of some abuses, contrary to established law, be meant by the word " reform;" unless the substitution, for an uncapable and abdicated prince, of him who was immediate heir to the other, and by the established law had a claim to the succession, can be considered as a radical change; unless a complete recurrence to all the provisions of the ancient and unimpaired constitution of the country, properly deserves the name of revolution; a name attributed to such an event by our English historians, when the word was not significant of all that which will hereafter render it a name of horror.

The governments of the continent of Europe were all gradually formed out of those feudal institutions in which the power of the paramount chief had originally more splendor than solidity. The privileges of the nobles, and the territorial lords, were a perpetual check upon all the encroachments of the sovereign, and not unfrequently upon the exercise of his legitimate prerogative. The barons were the great council of the nation, individually claiming a natural equality with their supreme head, and collectively asserting a constitutional superiority to his authority[*]. In the progress of commercial opulence, the commons acquired in many countries a share, and in

---

[*] " We," said the Justiza of Arragon, in the name of the nobility to the king, when they swore allegiance to him," who are each of us so good as you, and are altogether more powerful than you, promise obedience to your government, if you maintai   ·d · ·   · t · · ·   ·   but ·r's Revol.

some a full and adequate proportion of the legislative function. Thus, in none of those states was the original constitution that of a despotic monarchy, the prerogative of the prince being subject to restraint and limitation, by a power, at least equivalent to his own.

But the royal prerogative being uniformly exerted, and the powers of the nobles being less tolerable than that of the sovereign, whose undivided sway was to the great mass of the community a refuge from the oppression and exactions of a number; the assemblies of the states fell into general disuse, and the great kingdoms were consolidated under the uncontrouled government of a monarch.

In all these kingdoms the government of the monarch, though without the controul of those assemblies which had originally exercised a large portion of the public authority, was yet subject to the fundamental laws of the constitution; the authority of the states, though disused, was not obsolete; though not in exercise, was never abandoned by the nation nor disavowed by the crown. So that whatever occasion might arise in any of them to ameliorate the constitution, to improve the condition of society, to limit more strictly the royal prerogative, or to change any of the established institutions, there was never wanting a power in the constitution lawfully to effect all those purposes, and fully competent, when brought into action, to give and secure to the people the full enjoyment of practical liberty.

The Spanish monarchy was composed of many nations which had never, even in form, been united by the feudal bond, but which, by various accidents of conquest and succession, had passed under the domination of the same sovereign. Spain never enjoyed one supreme legislative assembly acting for the whole nation. Its assemblies of the Cortes were all of provincial authority, and its provinces had various laws and privileges, with no institution, in common, but that of the government of an hereditary monarch.

Such being the constitution of the Spanish monarchy, the crown had acquired a vast prerogative, not subject to any immediate practical check, from an efficient national legislative assembly; but it was nevertheless, bound by all the fundamental rules of the original feudal constitution, variously modified by the peculiar institutions of the respective provinces.

In England, previous to the abdication of King James, there was an actual suspension of the constitutional powers. The crown had become subject to the influence of a foreign potentate. The functions of parliament had been usurped by the reigning prince, who attempted in violation of the essential principles of the government to suspend the established laws, to abrogate the Protestant religion, to violate the chartered privileges of his people, to evade the trial by jury, to rule without the aid of legislative counsel, to raise an independent revenue, and to exercise the powers of an absolute sovereign. Thus circumstanced, our ancestors, in that great crisis of their affairs, took refuge in the ancient principles of the British constitution.

King James fled from the wrath of his awakened subjects; the executive power was wholly lost; an efficient member of the legislature was wanting; there was a breach in the constitution.

The three orders of the realm instantly assembled in convention. They resolved that King James, " having endeavoured to subvert the con" stitution of the kingdom, by breaking the ori" ginal contract between king and people, and " having, by the advice of Jesuits, and other

" wicked persons, violated the fundamental laws,
" and withdrawn himself out of the kingdom, he
" had abdicated the government, and the throne
" was thereby become vacant." This was their
preliminary step to that act by which they conferred the crown upon King William and Queen Mary; she being the next in the line of succession to the late king, and to the infant prince of Wales, who was incapable of exercising the powers of government, and whom his father had taken out of the realm to be educated in those principles of arbitrary power and superstition, which were found incompatible with the principles of the English monarchy.

The Spanish nation was recently placed in circumstances certainly far more difficult and perilous, but in kind resembling those which this country experienced in 1688.

In the constitution of that monarchy, composed of several independent kingdoms, the principles of ancient freedom, though far more obscure than in our constitution, were yet sufficiently legible. Civil liberty was their original birth-right and possession, and was the corner stone of their national establishment, though it had never been assimilated and combined, as it was at an early period in this country, with all the principles of a pure jurisprudence, an enlightened legislation, a liberal national religion, and the various institutions of an improved civil polity. Their freedom, though ancient and indubitable, was, in its best days, that of a community not perfectly associated, and having to acquire, rather than to enjoy, the complicated advantages of a government, strong by the laws which it enforces, and by the liberties which it protects.

Spain had not the advantages which we derive from our insular situation. Whatever differences have arisen in our state, either among contending parties, or between the different orders of the commonwealth, they have been determined without the intervention of foreign force, or the influence of any other government. In the dissensions of the rival families of Lancaster and York; in the grand rebellion, when parliament opposed itself to the king's prerogative; and at the change of 1688, when the whole nation was in resistance to the misguided and bigotted tyranny of King James, no armies were sent from abroad to controul the national will, or to promote a cause adverse to our general interests. In Spain it has been otherwise. The Pyrenean mountains have proved no barrier against the intrigues or attacks of a foreign potentate. Long before the demise of Charles III. the counsels of that monarchy were controuled by foreign influence. At the failure of his line, the disputed succession was settled, after a long war, by the military force of France, which has since, with little interruption, maintained its undue controul over all the affairs of that country. We now observe with what peculiar difficulty and hazard an independency from that galling yoke can be asserted by the Spanish nation.

Since the accession of the Bourbon line to the Spanish throne, the royal family yielded vassalage to the monarchy of France, and assumed an indifference to the public will of its own subjects, alike inconsistent with the grandeur and riches of the inheritance, and with the ancient laws and spirit of that nation. In all her foreign relations, Spain was identified with France. To that disgraceful alliance were sacrificed the dignity of the crown, the interests and wishes of the people, even the forms of the constitution, and almost the name of independence. Weakened, and urged, restrained by the fear and hatred of the popular will, and bound by the force of the established vassalage, not even the French revolution, and the slaughter of the elder branch of the royal line could stimulate the court of Madrid to break the fetters of its bondage. After a feeble resistance to the new power raised in France, it passed almost voluntarily to a humiliation and servitude far more oppressive than that which it had long borne; because its new servitude was imposed by a tyranny far more relentless, and violated the sense of honor, the ties of natural affinity, the hopes of Europe, the plainest interests of the state, and the universal security of all nations.

That last humiliation was marked by the rule of a low-born unprincipled favourite, whose undeserved elevation the influence of France sustained. He displayed his authority by arrogance and pride, such as great and unexpected promotion is apt to generate in a vulgar mind. The King and the Queen, like gilded puppets, appeared, and spoke, and acted as he the manager of the drama directed them. The heir to the monarchy he kept in obscurity and inaction. The great nobles of the realm he degraded and insulted, the laws of the state he violated, its treasures he squandered with wanton profusion, the means of its defence and potency he sacrificed in unnecessary and fatal warfare. He committed spoil upon the revenues of the church, he trampled upon the lives and fortunes of the lower orders, he sent away the military force upon distant expeditions, inconsistent with any sound policy, and introduced into the heart of the country, hordes of a foreign soldiery to maintain him in his exercise of authority which every Spaniard detested and despised. Such was the overbearing power of the proud minion, that he arrogated to himself the rights and the splendor of royalty, and made the sovereign a mere instrument of his administration.

By his misrule and boundless pretensions, dissatisfaction and hatred were excited in every mind; there appeared, through the whole nation, a disposition to revolt. The king's authority was reduced to absolute insignificance. The heir to the throne, whom the favourite had injured, insulted, and reviled, was beloved on that account, and for the vigorous and patriotic policy which he openly approved. The nobles, and the people looked to him as a leader in the approaching crisis, which the folly and the excesses of the upstart rapidly accelerated. The gathering storm was about to burst, in which the King could only depend for succour upon the French government, for whose service he had lost the affections of all his people. He was unwilling to oppose himself, with such aid, and in such a cause, to the indignation and resentment of the nation, and hoped, by abdication, to avert every danger.

But the emperor of France foresaw that the government of Ferdinand would have no resemblance to the pusillanimous misrule of his predecessor. By anticipation, he saw the youthful monarch stimulated and assisted by a gallant nobility to regain the independence of his crown; and already trembled, lest the efforts and example of a patriot king of Spain should limit that universal empire, which he labours to establish, or ultimately shake the foundations of that throne from which he issues his mandates to the prostrate nations.

When the great interests of the present eventful period shall be overwhelmed in the current of time, when the majesty of empire shall no longer cast a fallacious splendor upon atrocious usurpation, and the abasement of misfortune shall not lessen the due honour and estimation, of suffering merit; whenever it shall be important to display the natural deformity of injustice, cruelty, and treachery, for purposes of useful example, and to excite a noble emulation in the infant breast, by recounting deeds of heroic resolution and manly enterprise, accomplished by patriots in defiance of danger and difficulty for their lawful and glorious purposes; then will the historian dwell upon all the circumstances of the present awful crisis, in the affairs of Spain. Hatred and indignation will accompany his long recital, from the first interference of the tyrant, till the consummation of his perfidy by the imprisonment of his royal victims at Bayonne. The simple and explicit relation of Don Pedro Cevallos may be his guide and instruction. At present every incident of the complicated scheme is impressed upon the heart, and it would be an unnecessary task to enumerate all the crimes and artifices which, at length, excited the resentment of all Spaniards, and occasioned their resistance to the aggressors, of the common enemy of all established government.

The successful issue of that complicated scheme was the second abdication of the monarchy by the late king, a compelled abandonment of his title by Ferdinand, (whose right was immediate upon the abdication of his father) and a proclamation of Joseph, the revolutionary king of Naples, and the brother of the tyrant of France.

In this emergency the Spanish nation closely pursued the steps of the English, at their memorable change of 1688. Their late king had made a formal abdication; they generously rested upon that circumstance, and avoided the painful necessity of a judicial scrutiny of the errors, or the faults of his government. Though there was abundant evidence " of his having endeavoured

" to subvert the constitution of his kingdom by
" breaking the original contract between king and
" people, and by having violated the fundamental
" laws," yet with moderation, similar to that of our
convention, they thought it sufficient to recognise his abdication, and to acknowledge the accession of Ferdinand.

That great national proceeding was not the act of the irritated mob of the capital, goaded by oppression to tumult and to massacre, and taking the name of their unfortunate prince as a watchword for union, in a business of popular insurrection. In that case, all the dignity of the transaction would have been wanting; nor would it have rested upon those principles of honor, justice, and public virtue, which claim our applause and co-operation. Then the tocsin would have once more affrighted us as a signal for new outrages, pillages, and murders. The idol of the rights of the people again instated in his polluted sanctuary, must have been again appeased by appropriate victims; the work of confiscation, proscription, calumny, and judicial slaughter would have proceeded in the ferocious excesses of a capricious, cruel, and tumultuous sedition. Then should we have heard that all the orders of distinction were abolished, and that the inheritance of the church was seized by rapacious hands for the use of the emancipated nation; that religious sentiment was extinguished, and moral restraint disowned; that the laws and ordinances of justice were lost in the provisions of an ostentatious declaration of unfounded rights; that the executioner was already weary in the exercise of his liberalized functions under those provisions; that terror and destruction had loosened every tie of affinity and friendship, and that the passions, which always triumph in treason and rebellion, were raging with the honored attributes of authority. Then it might have been said, without a gross violation of historic truth, that there was "an insurrection "of the common people, of the middle, and, "above all, of the lower orders;" "that the bulk, "the mass of the people, the very odious many "headed beast, the multitude, the mob itself, had "raised the standard of insurrection, and had "borne it through massacre and through victory." Then might some men have exulted in that massacre, and that victory; "as a grand and perma- "nent success, as a lesson to all governments, a "warning to all oligarchies, and a cheering ex- "ample to every people."

But in that case the English nation would have felt a less universal sympathy with the motives and the object of that enterprise. We should have paused before we united in action and interest with such an ally as " the multitude "or the mob;" of any country whatsoever, in any cause. Those principles of order to which we have hitherto adhered in many vicissitudes of fortune, and in the support of which we have laboured for the rescue of all Europe from its depression under a power founded in their destruction, we should not have abandoned on slight political considerations. Strenuously contending against those who attribute the formation and the permanence of all rightful government to such fearful anarchy, there are those among us who would not have sacrificed the moral question of the contest to the precarious advantage which turbulent and unlawful power might have promised; there are those who would prefer to fall under the sword of the usurper, rather than adopt any step which would legalize the revolution by such confederacy.

It is not the irritated mob to whom we attribute that grand proceeding of the universal Spanish nation. In every province of the kingdom there was formed a junta, composed of whatever was most respectable for rank, property, energy, talent, character, and moral consideration. Those base courtiers, who were the creatures of the favorite, could not participate in the labour or the glory of that cause. The public functionaries whom he had made the tools of his corrupt administration, who had helped "to ren-"der necessary the effusion of blood, and had al-"most rendered it vain," were necessarily excluded from the patriotic duty. But we may rejoice for the honor of the ancient nobility of Europe, that the nobles of Spain had their full weight and consideration in the national councils. When we read the names of Infantado, the Palafoxes, Florida Blanca, Romana, and many other dignitaries who would augment the lustre of any chivalrous body in the best days of society; when we recollect that the governors of the great towns, the commanders of the fleets, and the leaders of the armies, gave their earliest support to the principles of that cause, and became its distinguished leaders, we rejoice that, although "the "herd of titled intriguers, who had misruled the "monarchy, and had deserted it in its utmost "need," had fled from their posts; to receive the reward of crime and treachery in the court of the foreign usurper; there, like the profligate suitors at the palace of Ulysses, converted into a house of riot, at the expence of the rightful exiled king

"To feast, to dance, and raise the mirthful song;"

yet there remained a great mass of the honor and consideration of the land which had never participated in that crime, and would perish in the noble cause which they espouse, rather than abandon their fidelity to their only lawful lord.

In that suspension of the powers of government, the provincial assemblies, without discussing one revolutionary question; without making one change in the political order of the state; without assuming a right to make such change, proceeded to restore the various authorities in the departments of justice; of finance, and of the public force. Having no object in view but to save the country, and to call forth its utmost energies in that day of peril, they happily concurred in that resolution which, if their motives had not been altogether patriotic, or if there had been among them the least particle of vanity, selfishness, ambition, or pride, they would never have entertained. They ordered the convocation of a supreme central junta; which was to decide the fate of the country, if that decision could be made by any civil authority.

The central junta assembled and became the point of union for the patriotism, the loyalty, and the valour of all Spain. Their declarations of rights were not like the inflamed manifestos, fabricated in the commune of Paris, and at Chalkfarm; they were unaffected, rational, and dutiful. They will hereafter be the best examples to be observed by every great nation that shall be warlike, without being unjust, and be in patriotic commotion without disorder or licentiousness. Their first measure was to ratify the title of king Ferdinand VII. In his name they proceeded to exercise the powers of majesty, and to confirm every fundamental principle and institution of the Spanish monarchy.

If there was any division of the public sentiment of the Spanish nation at that crisis, if the expression adopted by his Britannic majesty of the universality of the patriotic feeling will not be hereafter adopted by him who shall record the circumstances of that eventful period, still the statement of the Edinburgh reviewers will not pass into the historic page. It will be remembered that, upon that important question, there were on the one side the abdicated king and his queen; the crafty minister, to whose crimes and intrigues the national calamities will be charged; and the abandoned creatures of that minister, few in number, decorated with undeserved honors, still devoted to that cause of indignity and bondage in which alone they can hope for distinction, and always prepared, for base reward, to sacrifice their sovereign and the state. On the other side was the youthful monarch, languishing in the imprisonment of the relentless tyrant, who, like the malignant monster, imagined in romantic fable, betrayed even kings to his treacherous hospitality, and by magic force retained them to be the slaves of his guilty grandeur. Then came the hereditary nobles, the magistracy, the clergy, the whole of the ancient military force, and whatever could constitute the public will, territorial and commercial. All those, pure in honor and faithful to duty, were united with the antique spirit of knighthood, to break the adulterate spell of their detested enemy, to liberate his royal victim, to restore the ancient glory of their dejected country, and to bear the standard of heroic virtue till it waves triumphantly in the courts of that same gloomy castle where their king was circumvented by wicked artifice. Subordinately to all those was the aristocracy of talents, not there prostituted to the service of faction, nor attempting to justify the atrocious actions of the usurper. Far less enthuslastic at that time was the multitude, then almost deaf at the call of loyalty, or coming slowly forward to recruit the armies of the legitimate government, and to participate in their proper function for the overthrow of an odious despotism under which all orders would groan alike.

" Whether Ferdinand or Charles be the mo-
" narch," the Edinburgh reviewers " care not, or
" whether a new stock be brought from Germany
" for a breed." The allusion to our English royalty is not obscure. To them that personal attachment to the prince which makes submission noble, which results from confidence and benefits experienced, which introduces every domestic affection into our public relations, which makes the obligation of social life as the filial tribute which a virtuous mind delights to pay, and renders the splendor of power a common property and consideration; for that loyalty of the heart, these philosophic speculators care not at all. The lineage, the character, the temper, and the mental qualities of the reigning family are to them unworthy of regard. " That the Spaniards should have a
" king, every one must admit, who believes that
" an hereditary monarch, well fettered by the con-
" stitution, is the best guardian of civil liberties."
They leave the question undecided, whether any monarch is wanted for that guardianship; but if he be admitted upon any terms, " he must be well
" fettered by the constitution, he must be suffici-
" ently controuled in the exercise of his delegated
" and responsible trust;" and being well fettered, and sufficiently controuled, who the monarch is, whether he be Charles, who has ruined and betrayed the state, or Ferdinand, his legitimate and beloved successor, or one of a German race; whether he be wise or weak, just or cruel, brave

or pusillanimous, an elected or an hereditary prince, it signifies nothing to them. Provided the people retain "an universal feeling of their "own powers," they little care. The cause which they have advocated will then triumph and be permanent; the king holding his trust and dignity at the caprice of the multitude, having no independent prerogative, insulted, every day by the remonstrances of those to whom he is responsible, and reminded every hour that he has but a delegated function; this pennyless, impotent, dishonoured phantom of royalty, the creature of a factious, restless, insolent, omnipotent democracy, of merely nominal consideration, may slumber, or may rage with powerless indignation upon his civic throne. His subjects will keep alive "the "recollection of their great actions," and be always alert "to shake to atoms every intrigue "hostile to their imputed rights."

But the monarchy to which they will assent would be of short duration. A wise sovereign, claiming by succession and by legal title, will naturally feel that the first duty of his office is to promote the greatness and the happiness of the people, and that by the discharge of that duty he will most augment the splendor of his crown, and the solidity of his power, and will perpetuate the inheritance to his children's children. In the exercise of his prerogative, strengthened and defined, but not reduced, impoverished, and opposed by the prudent provisions of the law, he will not find himself in every act of government curtailed of all judgment and discretion by the paramount privileges of a jealous commonalty. He will feel, that, unlike inferior functionaries, he has a nobler duty to perform, than that of a literal execution ice, prudence, and public principle, which are all of them expressive of a liberal discretion, must naturally be the objects of his high ministration. These combined, but not restrained, by a faithful observance of the constitutional rights of all the orders of the state will, at once, appear to him as his dignified interest and imperious duty.

The prince, who is no more than a factitious magistrate, who is fettered and controuled in every act of national beneficence and generous speculation, whose natural object it must be to destroy that constitution over which another power presides, and which he is not called upon to protect, who must always regard his people with the fear of dependant impotence, or the hatred of jealous rivalship; such a prince may be suited to the philosophy of speculative short-sighted reformers; but he is not suited to the grandeur and generosity of an opulent and magnanimous nation. His existence, permitted, and not necessary, ostentatious and not useful, will be of precarious, unquiet, and short duration; the form of the government will hastily verge towards the character of absolute democracy, or be changed to an ungracious and unqualified despotism. If he be of a firm, persevering, enterprising, cruel, and relentless ambition, he will soon triumph over the restraints of law, and establish in his own person an unbending, uncontrouled supremacy. If he be meek and gentle, easily entreated, upright and forgiving, true to his engagements, and more averse to the shedding the blood of the rebellious than to the diminution of his feeble authority, then, like Louis XVI., he will yield his life upon the scaffold to infuriated traitors, and the destruction of his power will make way for a sanguinary, merciless, and upstart usurpation.

Though the efforts of patriotism, assisted by the counsel and protection of this country, should unhappily fail of saving the Peninsula from the unrelaxing gripe of the usurper, the Spanish monarchy may yet survive in its opulent and extensive dependencies. The royal house of Portugal yet reigns in its transatlantic territories, and has afforded an example which ought not to be unavailing to the Government of Spain. In that case, the question with respect to the colonies in South America will not be, as the Edinburgh reviewers have stated, "whether they shall remain as be- "fore, attached to that monarchy, or, in other "words, shall become the property of Napoleon, "or whether those colonies under the protection of "Great Britain shall be enabled to constitute them- "selves a free and independent nation."* The question will be whether or not we shall sustain the rightful title of King Ferdinand to those possessions, or " become a party to revolution- "ary measures," and support the cause of jacobinism in the new world.

An affected dread of the power of France is expressed by the reviewers; but their counsel, whatever it might be, is founded on an opinion laboriously inculcated, that none but revolutionary principles can be opposed to that power with any hope of success. Instead of being an honest ally of Ferdinand, to whom we have pledged our faith, they require us to assimilate our policy to that of the usurper. He has claimed the crown; we are counselled to destroy its prerogative. He strives to possess its

* See the number of the Edinburgh Review page 199.

European territories; we are to revolutionize those in America. We, under the mask of alliance, are to perpetrate a crime which hostility would not justify, and to inflict a more deadly blow upon the rights of the Spanish royalty, than the avowed enemy has presumed to denuntiate.

The progress of human affairs announces to the philosophic eye a great revolution, the nature and consequences of which the boldest imagination cannot calculate. The new world, advancing in population, science, and civilization, will not always continue in dependance upon the states of Europe. The establishment of the federal republic, and the emancipation of San Domingo, are but a commencement of that change which will hereafter give a new direction to the policy of all nations, and open new sources of power and intelligence. The wrongs of the untaught natives of Mexico and Peru will, probably, at no distant day, be retributed by mighty states, which will be established on the separation of those vast provinces from the countries which subdued them. Time which can effectuate, without violence, those transitions which the rash precipitancy of mankind cannot produce without accumulated evils, will, in due course, loosen the fetters of subjection which bind the nations of America. Even to the poor Indian shall be imparted the blessings of knowledge, liberty, and power. A wise man would not wish to wrest to himself the management of the important work. An attempt to do so will originate in presumption, be executed in crime, and, whatever may be the ultimate result, must terminate in immediate calamity.

If France should accomplish her purpose of

conquering Spain, the American colonies will appertain by sound principles of justice to Ferdinand, or the lawful claimant of his house. An independence will then be insured to the provinces without revolution, and the usurper, acquiring the immediate object of his ambition, will be without the golden prize which impelled his cupidity. The object of the Edinburgh Reviewers will be equally frustrated. The republican example of the United States of America which dazzles their eye, will not have been followed, and revolution in the spirit of loyalty and honour will, in their view, be without merit or commendation.

One favourable result from the resistance of Spain to the wanton enmity of France, cannot be lost to mankind. Whatever may be the immediate result of the contest, her great example will remain to animate the nations, apparently in hopeless bondage, to assert their independence. The hostile spirit of those countries, which have an habitual hatred to the domination of France, though broken, cannot be annihilated. Italy, the states of Germany, and Russia, must be indignant at their common humiliation. Though as yet they may be unable to renew the contest with their cruel conqueror, yet a day must come, when they will again appeal to arms. The power of France founded in error will be shaken to its base, if the people on the continent should acquire an opinion that her armies are not invincible.

It is not necessary to extract the whole of the illustrations and applications of the doctrine already quoted from the Edinburgh Reviewers, and continued through fourteen closely printed pages of their number published in October. The whole of that article seems to refer to England rather than to Spain. In the domestic state of the English gov... ... ...ign

policy. They exult " that they can now once
" more utter the word *liberty* and people, without
" starting at the echo of their own voices, or
" looking round the chamber for some spy or
" officer of government; they anticipate a most
" salutary change in public opinion, from the ex-
" ample of Spain." They state that " the Spanish
" Revolution places the cause of freedom and
" reform upon a much better footing than it had
" even at the beginning of the French Revolution,
" because the country, government, and people,
" are committed with the Spanish Patriots, which
" they never were with those of France;" they
observe, " that the cause of the Spaniards is so
" obviously that of the people, the desertion of
" the court and nobles is so manifest; the con-
" nexion between the success of the patriots and
" a radical change of the government is so neces-
" sary, that whoever has wished well to them
" feels intimately persuaded that he has been es-
" pousing the popular side of the greatest question
" of the present day, that he has been praying
" most fervently for the success of the people
" against their rulers; that he has in plain terms
" been as far as in him lay, a party to revolu-
" tionary measures;" " that he has admitted the
" right of the people to call their rulers to account
" and choose their own constitution;" " men of all
" descriptions, of all ranks in society, of every party,
" have joined almost unanimously in the same
" generous and patriotic sentiments, and have ex-
" pressed them loudly and manfully;" " the nation
" has formally taken part in the cause of Spain,"
" after recognizing in the most solemn manner the
" revolutionary government." " They sincerely
" believe that the success of that cause would
" not o   ave the continent, but w   intel'ib'y

" purify the internal constitution both of this and
" the other countries of Europe." "They would
" extravagantly rejoice in any conceivable event,
" which must reform the constitution of England,
" by reducing the overgrown influence of the
" crown, by curbing the pretensions of the privi-
" leged orders in so far as this can be effected,
" without strengthening the royal influence, by
" raising up the power of real talents and work,
" the true nobility of a country, by exalting the
" mass of the community, and giving them under
" the guidance of that virtual aristorcracy, to
" direct the councils of England." "Whoever be-
" lieves that an event leading to such glorious
" consequences as these, would not give them the
" most heartfelt joy, must have read but few of
" the pages of their journal, or profited but little
" by what he has read."

There are doctrines advanced and ably supported in earlier Publications of the Edinburgh
Review which have no resemblance to the principles here detailed. Those who have read their
former political treatises and profited by what they
read, will be astonished at the apparent inconsistency of sentiment, which now expresses heartfelt
joy at that prospect of revolution, from which in
1807, those same reviewers anticipated little, "but
" general degradation and misery; and stepped
" beyond the limits of their duty to express their
" horror at the suggestion, and to contribute their
" aid to rouse and to undeceive those who may
" have been misled by different anticipation."*
An attempt will be made in the course of these
pages, to exhibit "some instances of what has
" certainly appeared as a most glaring and out-
" rageous contradiction;"* and what is of far more

* 10 E. B. Review of Cobbett.

importance to inquire whether the effects of the new doctrines of the Review "are likely to be "pernicious or salutary, to detect what is dele- "terious in the nostrum that is just handing out "among the multitude, and to exhibit an antidote "to the poison of which the doses are at this "moment making up."*

While they maintained any character for loyalty, and confined themselves to that censure of the operations of government, which in a free country must always be tolerated, though it was much lamented that their discussions of public questions contained little justice or moderation, yet the effect of them was not greatly dreaded: though their argument was neither sound nor generous, yet its fundamental principles were not plainly adverse to the constitution of the country: though they wandered far in the licentiousness of political debate, and censured the measures of ministers without civility or reserve, yet they abstained from an open denial of the rights of the established government, and were not argumentatively opposed to the principles of the English Monarchy, or of English Liberty. Happily they have cast aside the veil which obscured the mysterious secrets of their doctrine. They imagined that the Spanish cause was revolutionary, and that its principles were adopted by the English nation; as if touched by the spear of Ithuriel; "up they start discovered;" they abandon the reptile form of concealment, in which they whispered seductive casuistry to our disordered fancy, and in the terrific magnitude of their natural form, like the first apostate, they disclose their whole design and treachery; with haughty disdain they revile and censure the

* Review of Cobbett.

superior powers which hitherto they had feared; they appear the bold assertors of revolutionary freedom; they offer their public homage to the principles of the French Rebellion, and to the principles which they falsely impute to the Spanish Insurrection; in unequivocal language they fervently pray for the success of the people against their rulers; their rhapsody of declamation they apply to the constitution of England; they proclaim themselves of that party which is for reducing the influence of the crown, for curbing the pretensions of the nobles, and for establishing the philosophic rule of the mass of the community under the guidance of an aristocracy of talents. It is happy that they gallantly stand forth in declared hostility to the existing powers of the state; and that all pretence of admonitory censure and deceitful counsel is laid aside:

> "An open foe may prove a curse,
> "But a pretended friend is worse."

END OF PART I.

THE RIGHTS OF THE SOVEREIGNTY.

PART THE SECOND.

THE Edinburgh Reviewers "would extravagantly "rejoice in any conceivable event which should "raise up the power of talents and worth, the true "nobility of a country, and exalt the mass of the "community by giving them under the guidance of "that virtual aristocracy to direct the councils of "England." A principle similar to this prevailed in France twenty years ago. It is worthy of inquiry whether reason or experience will induce us to sympathize with this wish of the Edinburgh Reviewers, in favour of the aristocracy of talents.

The progress of political opinion in the states of civilized Europe may be traced from its earliest origin, when governments resulted from the personal choice of the rude warriors, in a sort of martial election, to that happier period when liberty was fixed in the provisions of jurisprudence, and power was rendered sacred and independent by the authority of law. Under the fostering care of a learned and opulent superstition, science had escaped from the rigourous bondage of the darker ages, and was majestically seated in the seminaries of education. Her pupils, honorably endowed by the munificence of pious and liberal founders, were no longer solicitous of the dole of private bounty, and pursued their useful labours in academic tranquillity and unassuming independence. From that dignified retirement, they were called to accomplish the plans of enlightened monarchs, and to ameliorate the condition of mankind, by a wise and temperate application of the principles of practical legislation to the fundamental ordinances of the state.

Favoured and honorably employed by the princes whom they served, and revered by the great mass of the community, whose duties they illustrated, and whose interests they promoted, these eminent personages, as law-givers, as magistrates, as divines, and as statesmen, in the unrestrained exercise of their distinguished functions, developed a great system of social philosophy, which undoubtedly gave a peculiar character to the ages in which they flourished. Into their hands the proudest monarchs yielded the rod of despotic power, and arbitrary kings submitting to their restraints, renounced the rights of conquest, claimed a better title than that of military prowess, and became the legal sovereigns of the nations which they ruled. Europe was for ever saved from that uncontrouled imperial sway, under which the Roman world had lain in subjection; much less danger was there of that feeble, sumptuous, and licentious effeminacy of royalty by which the eastern nations have been degraded in almost every age. By the influence of example and preceptive counsel, and by that persuasive authority which subdues the heart while it liberates and refines the manners of a savage race, they persuaded subjects that submission to the laws is not concession to force, but a civil obligation, and a principle of generous loyalty. The exercise of magistracy through their ministration was no longer sustained by the display of warlike array, but was secured by the inoffensive symbols of public justice. Obedience to beneficent authority was the result of virtuous principle and enlightened choice, and was entirely unmixed with that slavish terror, which tyrants only would inspire, and to which ignorance and vice only can submit.

The names of those illustrious sages, although they are not found in the temple of modern reason, nor in the margins of our books of the modern philosophy, are yet not wholly forgotten in the present great uproar of the world. The founders of that raging anarchy which has dissolved the ancient ties of society, and weakened the respect which the nations were accustomed to pay to Bacon and to More, to Grotius and to Puffendorf, to L'Hopital, to D'Argensseau, and to Pothier, and to the rest of the venerable series, which it would be tedious to enumerate, have not acquired a countervailing influence and authority, so universally predominant, but that there are those in every country, and many in the British Empire, who will yet render homage to their venerable names, and will defend the institutions which they established and adorned.

The maxim which was the deepest root of their philosophy, was that of practical improvement. They proceeded upon no system of experimental speculation, nor ever conceived an imaginary calculation of political advantages, balanced against moral evils, to justify counsel not immediately beneficial. Where any people was found in the restraint of a barbarous bondage, they invented laws to coerce the tyrannizing power. Where the arm of magistracy was too weak to restrain the licentiousness of crime, or to call forth the national energies in the time of peril, there they strengthened it by new prerogative. All abstract principle they avoided. The uniform tenor of their writings and their unvaried practice prove, beyond controversy, what was their opinion of such discussions; notorious grievances they exposed and ultimately redressed; actual abuses they censured and gradually remedied; not by violent innovation and subversion of subsisting institutions, but by bending the form of the established power to meet the new necessity. That power, whatever it was, they made the basis of good government; they supplied its defects, if any appeared, by novel applications of acknowledged principles; they corrected its excesses, whatever they were, by the authority of some undoubted provision of the original constitution, which they extended and defined to meet every novel exigency. Thus were all the crude and savage regulations of the primitive barbarians, who founded the European Commonwealth, converted into mild and beneficent institutions, in which the supremacy of the laws was paramount to all privilege, and the good of the community was the great purpose of government.

Society itself they considered as a natural institution, arising out of the primitive character of mankind, necessary to their tranquillity and safety, and ordained by that same providence which gave to the human race its intellectual dignity, with that sense of duty, universal love, and mutual obligation, which displays itself at the earliest dawn of reason. They did not consider man as sent into life for that dreary and precarious existence which has been imagined to precede the institutions of civil government. The rude savage who subsists by his individual strength, destitute of knowledge and intellectual power, timid, speechless, naked, and abandoned, a slave to the caprices of the seasons, the sport and prey of the beasts, which, like him, roam for slaughter, and are stronger though not more ferocious than himself; such a poor miserable, ignorant, incapable, forlorn, and hopeless wretch, they never thought fit to idolize as the founder of social philosophy, and the author of legal obligation; they never taught that their magnificent and humane institutions of national polity were established in the imaginary absurd convention of beings so base and comfortless as he; nor did they recognize in that extreme brutality and weakness, those natural rights of man which are proper to be the foundation of civil liberty.*

Therefore they adopted as a principle, that society was not a civil institution; but that, combined by some sort of jurisprudence under some form of government, it was coeval with the reason of mankind. They did not acknowledge that any possibility of right, or any pretension to power, could be derived in the social state, from that condition of savage independence, which licentious

* The learned reader will recollect an eloquent passage of Puffendorf, illustrative of the condition of savage man. lib 1. c. 3. "Fingamus hominem, citra omnem ab aliis hominibus accedentem curam et culturam, ad robustam ætatem provectum, cui nihil sit scientiæ, nisi quod ex proprio ingenio velut ultro pullulavit, eundemque ab omni aliorum ope atque consortio in solitudine destitutum. Sane vix miserabilius animal deprehendetur. Elingue nimirum, ac nudum, cui nihil aliud relictum quam herbas radicesque vellera aut sponte natos fructus legere, sitim fonte, flumine aut lacuna obvia levare, repellendis aeris injuriis antra subire, aut musco gramineve corpus utcunque tegere, tempus tædiosissimum per otium exigere, ad quemvis strepitum aut alterius animantis occursum exhorrescere, denique fame, frigore, aut per feram bestiam demum periturum."

imagination has pourtrayed as existing antecedently to the social union. The compact which prescribes the privileges and the duties of all the orders in a national confederation, they considered as formed in the social state, and not as prior to its constitution; and they never conceived that any interpretation of that compact or any assumption of rights anterior to its establishment, and independent of its provisions, could release the civilized man from its obligations or deprive him of its protection, like "the unaccommodated man, " which is no more than a poor, bareforked animal."

The social compact was a law and a bond of union, to ascertain and confirm the powers and prerogatives of the different orders, to ensure their respective advantages, to enforce their reciprocal duties, and to hold them in mutual dependance. To every order and individual it assigned its peculiar function, with responsibility to the law, and without any right to violate and to destroy the function and privilege of any other order or individual. Every community of men is a great complex corporation, in which the supreme head exercises his superior function under the ascertained provisions of the social code, with royal dignity and independence, and he is bound to discharge the duties attached to his pre-eminence and power; every individual in his subordinate class has also his peculiar function, to be exercised in the exigences of the state, with corresponding privileges which are sacred in the law, and with duties which are essential to the wellbeing of the commonwealth.

In their social economy, every degree was integral and independent, from the monarch whose power and irresponsibility were the consummation of the complicated structure, to the hardy peasantry, whose lowliness was not despised in their regard to public happiness. Neither the monarch in his high elevation, nor the superior orders in their dignity and privilege, far less the mass of the peasantry, and the multitude, had any judicial function over the other constituted authorities, either for inquiry, chastisement, or correction. The penalties of jurisprudence are devised for personal offenders, and its process can only be directed against those who may be obnoxious to censure and to punishment; but the orders of the state acknowledge no tribunal competent to cite them to judgment, or to visit their malefactions in vengeance, or for example. The lower class is least of all endowed with such a power, although it possesses the largest portion of brute force, and is exceedingly numerous; because it is destitute of temperance and prudence, and is naturally disabled from exercising any constitutional function, except by agency and delegation. In their estimate of national rights, the usurpation of the prince, the insolence of presumptuous nobles, and the restless violence of an insurgent commonalty, were alike unlawful.

But their notions of public law had respect to the vicissitudes of temporal affairs, and to that frailty of our mortal nature which will contaminate the most provident institutions of human policy. Therefore they assigned to all the orders of the state, combined in legislative action, a power to make such changes of law as the exigencies of affairs might require; and they did not withhold from the sound and uncorrupted members of the commonwealth, acting in legislative union, the power of supplying for themselves a lawful chief, if by manifest transgression of the fundamental laws, or by unquestioned abdication, there should be a suspension of the supreme authority. The weak and demolished parts of the social fabric were at all times to be strengthened and restored; the folly or the crime of the presiding functionary was not to loosen the bond of society, nor to liberate men from all wholesome restraint to roam in anarchy till they might again be bound by legal obligation, or coalesce in orderly arrangement.

A sublimer branch of their philosophy held, that all communities of men are bound by a law superior to any social obligation, whether it be prescribed by the authority of paramount legislation, or result from implied convention. They considered that as in private life, no caprice of passion, no prospect of emolument, and no excess of resentment palliates a breach of the national law, so in the public relations, no certainty of immediate, far less a probability of contingent benefits can justify any member of the commonwealth in a violation of that universal law, which, for the good of mankind, has ordained the inviolable sanctity of constituted authority. That law of our nature may be traced to a divine original, if there be any principle which can be deduced from that sacred source. It is a rule applicable to all the relations of peace and war. It ordains that truth and justice shall direct us in every domestic and public transaction; that obedience and respect are a tribute due to those who exercise the powers of government; and that treachery, violence, and massacre are not less atrocious, as the measures of a powerful community in resistance to authority, than as the acts of lawless individuals.

These illustrious men were the companions and counsellors of princes, and the preceptors of their people. They flourished under that patronage which was not yet extended to the sciolist and logician. Their deep erudition and practical philosophy, tending to the improvement and instruction of mankind, procured for them active and honorable duty, for which they would have been less qualified by an ostentatious talent for speculation and declaiming. They were placed high in rank and function; not for qualities of imagination and moral experiment, but for those of a vigorous, sound, and upright understanding; capable of sustaining and adding new props to the fabric of the laws, and of strengthening the foundations of happiness and order upon which that fabric rests.

There was no splendor of station and no species of power to which these men bowed in servile homage. If they were required, by an usurping master, to acknowledge an unlawful title of domination, like More they would suffer on the scaffold, rather than be the slaves of the proud tyrant. If a lawless multitude exacted from them a more degraded adulation, like De Witte they would submit to the same fate, and calmly expire amid the insolent revilings of an outrageous, sanguinary mob.

The diffusion of literature, and the facility of acquiring a superficial knowledge of philosophy, the gradual refinement of the modern languages, and the wide extension of corrupted taste among all classes, though they may have been productive of some advantages, which it would be absurd to deny, or to lament, have not been of pure and unmixed benefit to mankind. The ancient languages have become rather the ornamental appendage of polite education than the foundation of solid and extensive learning. So great has been the change, that even in the superior classes, it is rare to meet with any one who has attempted even to peruse the writings of those great masters of knowledge, whose elaborate works are poorly supplied by the more elegant productions of this enlightened age. A flippant and unsubstantial literature is preferred to deep and useful science. This revolution of taste had begun before the conclusion of the seventeenth century, when, with the dogmatism of religious contest, and the pedantry of scholastic learning, science, morality, and religion, were likewise excluded from the circles of fashion which moved round the mistresses of the courts of London and Versailles. Imagination, licentiousness, and wit, were then permitted to exercise a marked controul in the councils of nations.

At that time was founded the republic of letters, in which all the dignity of rank and fortune was made subservient to the distinctions of authorship and poetry. Unfading laurels were tendered without the hazard of noble enterprize, or the labor of great acquirement, to such princes as would acknowledge that republic. Its favor was solicited by warriors, by magistrates, and by all ranks of people; and children were taught to hold the recompence of fame which they bestowed, in higher estimation than the political recompence which statesmen could confer. But not from princes alone did the members of that wide institution exact their suit and homage. The rewards of princes might be resumed at pleasure, and were enjoyed by a precarious and dependant tenure. They invented a more honorable, secure, and profitable vassalage, and conceived the idea of a new sovereignty to become triumphant by the warfare of political reformers, and to be administered by " an aristocracy of talents."

Ambition is an innate quality of the human mind. There is no station so low, and no understanding so abased, as not to be sometimes actuated by the love of personal consideration and the desire of power. The scholar, in his privacy, toils for popularity and fame. Much more ardent is the thirst of preeminence which impels the loquacious theorist and speculator; he lives but for the applause of those whom his doctrines have seduced; he is jealous of the honor which he sees conferred upon talents of which he thinks contemptuously, more useful though less glittering than his own; he despises the precedence which the wisdom of our ancestry confirmed to fortune and factitious rank: in the riot of his imagination he conceives himself qualified to wield the sceptre of dominion, and to direct the affairs of nations.

It was an early effort of the literary crew to cast into contempt whatever was most venerable for antiquity of institution or permanence of establishment. The frailties of princes, the profligacy of courtiers, the errors of ministers, and all the abuses, which are unhappily inseparable from power, however constituted, they made the perpetual theme of sarcastic observation, and studiously obscured the uses and the benefits which are derived from regular government. They obtruded upon the view whatever was offensive and impure, and concealed whatever was noble, moral, or ornamental. The safety of the monarch is endangered when he stands exposed to the public eye deprived of those robes of honor with which he was wisely invested to hide the weakness and defects of personal character. Those robes they defiled, and indignantly tore away to shew the vulgar, that like them, he was mortal and imperfect. And not from the sovereign alone did they strip the decent garniture of office; but the nobility, the priesthood, the magistracy, whatever was reverend, or of public service, they exposed in its natural frailty and nakedness, to be the scorn and ridicule of the pampered multitude. Every thing they reduced to the level of debased humanity, and exulted in the comparison of their own vain superiority to the powers which they degraded, and the dignities which they reviled.

History has created her tribunal to judge the actions and designs of princes without respect to their dignity of station, or to the brilliancy of their power. It is for the happiness of mankind that the tyrant, whose throne is surrounded by the victims of unbounded ambition, or whose empire is raised on the ruins of subjugated states, cannot long exult in that fallacious glory which his parasites and the companions of his guilt extol. In the records of the historic page, his crimes will be faithfully enumerated; and he will not be permitted to claim that respect which is due only to virtue and beneficence; nor shall his name be enrolled among the benefactors of mankind. The judgment of history will be impartial, unsolicited by faction and conspiracy, and unbiassed by the facetiousness of humour or the treacherous illusions of interested eloquence. Such judgment cannot pass upon the living monarch. His own subjects are incapable of the necessary inquiry; because the respect which is due to his power and prerogative will not allow them to entertain the accusation; and the safety of society will not tolerate a jurisdiction before which the necessary evidence could be aduced and indifferently weighed. A claim to such jurisdiction will be always an instrument of treason, or the excuse of prejudiced disaffection. Much less to be tolerated is that unspecific accusation in which conspirators alone can indulge, though it is issued from the press in the form of critical research or periodical political observation.

If all governments were annihilated, and men were liberated from the coercion of human justice, to obey the impulses of passion, and to gratify the lusts of corrupted nature; yet if the reverence of almighty power, which most effectually controuls the wandering of desire and the excess of appetite, should not be obliterated from the mind, if the fear of future judgment should interpose to stay the hand of guilt, or if the restraints of morality should remain to correct the tumultuous principles of selfish independence; men would soon be weary of savage liberty, and would revert to some form of jurisprudence for their mutual safety and correction. The original founders of revolution perceived, that while the dread of a superior providence, or a belief in immortality, or a sense of moral obligation should influence society, so long the authority of human laws (which seems to be reduced from a nobler origin than human wisdom) would be respected by mankind. Their earliest attack therefore was against religion. They first assailed the christian revelation by serious argument and sarcastic ridicule. Then in treatises of deep philosophy they disputed and denied a creative power, attempted to prove the eternity of the universe, and attributed the harmony of the natural world, without any acknowledgment of the goodness and intelligence of a presiding deity, to the laws of mechanism and the necessary qualities of matter. Then they decried the established maxims of morality, and contended that all our social obligations are founded in general convention and in long experience of fitness and utility: lastly, they removed the only remaining principle of moral science, by casting into doubt, and disowning the immaterial existence of the soul, and that prospect of future retribution which is the only consolation of afflicted virtue, and the only terror of triumphant guilt. By this vast project of atheism and immorality to which they devoted the flights of genius, the speculations of science, the poignancy of satire, and the cunning ingenuity of reasoning, they hoped to invalidate the solid foundations of the social structure, and to prepare the minds of men for that influence of talent by which they hoped to be raised above the competition of power and the authority of religion.

The foundations of reverence and attachment being thus withdrawn from lawful government, they promulgated a new principle the most seductive that was ever tendered to a corrupted people. It was the doctrine of the rights of man, by which every subsisting establishment was reprobated as a flagrant usurpation, and the title of sovereignty was vested unalienably in the great mass of the people numerically taken. They asserted that all power is derived from that mass, that a majority might delegate and resume it at pleasure, and that no law or ordinance whatever can bind that majority. This principle invented by philosophers, who pretended to be lovers of concord, whose tears would flow at the carnage of war, and who bewailed the miseries of mankind with bitter lamentation, who professed to be destitute of all selfishness, meek, merciful, and unassuming, was edited as an integral maxim of the social compact, and it was instantly echoed in every country, as with the hundred voices of the Cumœan prophetess. Then was the commencement of revolution. Then the thrones of kings tottered upon their base. Then might have been predicted the subsequent events of that process of insurrection, the course of which cannot yet be limited. To that malignant hour we may attribute the calamities which Europe has endured, and the triumph of that prodigious tyranny which threatens the civilized world.

This captivating dogma was proffered at a period when the popular mind was free from immediate interest and admirably prepared for its reception. The controversies of the reformation had ceased to occupy its attention. On one side the spirit of religious persecution was extinct; on the other an indifference to the truth had succeeded to sectarean zeal. The perfect settlement of the balance of power, and the tranquil disposition of the greater monarchies, had allayed the heat of national rivalship. The progress of commercial opulence, and the general prosperity of Europe, had created a new class of men desirous of political consideration, who were certainly too little favored in the strict establishments of the continent. That prosperity, and the example of the great, at the same time, afforded the pernicious means of luxury, and created a general taste for pleasure and dissipation. A relaxation of manners which removed all reproach from profligacy and vice, had ensued. The urbanity of polished life had introduced a spirit of equality which lowered the barriers of social distinction without making them less odious to those who wished to overleap them. Morality had long been without honor in the circles of rank and fashion; the obscene works of fancy, and the fallacious discussions of impure philosophy, which the men of letters carefully threw into common circulation, had contaminated the mass of society. The hateful demon of infidelity was no longer chained in a gloomy obscurity, or marked with detestation when he dared to obtrude himself upon public notice. He now appeared, smiling and facetious, in gay attire, and with gaudy ornament; he was caressed by princes and flattered at their courts; and was entertained with no less favor in the subordinate walks of life. Whoever was emulous of distinction for politeness, humour, contempt of prejudice, and liberality of sentiment, and above all, those who panted for literary reputation, were anxious to scoff at that which the virtuous and the wise adore, and to proclaim their predilection for the novel system which disowned revelation, and questioned the being of a God.

It was in a like conjuncture of affairs, and in a like temper of public mind, that an attempt at similar revolution was made for the destruction of the Roman commonwealth. The historian who related the object and the circumstances of that conspiracy, has detailed a corresponding laxity of morals and prevalence of impiety. To a nation sunk in profligacy, luxury, and disaffection, Catiline proclaimed the anti-social levelling principle. " Omnes quos flagitium, egestas, conscius ani-
" mus agitabat, hi Catilinæ proximi familiaresque
" erant." To them the Roman jacobin promised a reward not different from that which has more fatally seduced the nations in this latter age. " Quin
" igitur expergiscemini ? En illa, illa, quam sæpe
" optâstis, libertas: præterea divitiæ, decus, gloria
" in oculis sita sunt: fortuna ea omnia victoribus
" proemia posuit. Res, tempus, pericula, egestas,
" belli spolia magnifica, magis quam oratio mea, vos
" hortentur."

Had it not been that a great statesman, then charged with the destinies of the Roman world, foresaw and estimated the perils of that sedition, the crimes and calamities of the present day might not have been without example. His provident and capacious mind detected the danger and prepared the remedy. His undaunted virtue over-awed those corrupted senators who were friendly to the principles of the insurrection, and presumed to ridicule his apprehensions. His firmness and perseverance were a terror to the public enemy, and eventually vanquished all resistance; to him his grateful country was indebted that she was not overwhelmed by treason and democratic faction at that awful crisis.

But during a whole century, Europe produced no such statesman, to ascertain a peril far more evident; and beyond calculation more tremendous. There were indeed a few private, powerless characters, whose sagacity perceived the approaching conflict; but they, like the Trojan prophetess, were inspired in vain.

"Tunc etiam fatis aperit Cassandra futuris
"Ora, Dei jussu non unquam credita Teucris."

But there was not one sovereign in Europe with prudence to observe the gathering tempest, and with courage to provide against its fury. Posterity shall be perplexed with fearful astonishment, to know that kings were the pupils and the nursing patrons of those philosophers who since have hurled them from their thrones. They shall hear with alarm that the jargon of equality, and the rights of man, disguised in song and folly, and passing by the names of philanthropy and freedom of opinion, was an exercise of elocution among the descendants of the hardy warriors who purchased their honorable distinction by virtue and by valour. They shall learn with surprize and indignation, that ministers of state, grave counsellors, and magistrates bearing the sword of justice, were content to be eulogized by those crafty preachers of sedition whom they ought to have suppressed and punished. The virtue of one individual saved Rome from impending ruin. Unhappy Europe shall attribute her downfal to the pusillanimity, the blindness, and the treachery of those who, entrusted with her safety, might have detected the conspirators in preparing that vast mine which burst at last with a ruinous and irresistible explosion.

The rebellion against the king of France was triumphant, and the rights of the people brought into actual exercise, by the men of letters and philosophers; by those successful rebels who established " une constitution qui a eu la perfidie d'exclure du premier rang l'intrigue et l'opulence, pour y placer deux divinites long temps obscures, *le talent et la vertu.*"* And then under the immediate guidance of the aristocracy of talents was practically promulgated, in aid of the political dogma, a moral doctrine, without which the project of the revolution might have failed. The necessity of the case occasioned the horrid monstrous conception. Like the portentous progeny of the arch-fiend, it was the natural generation of that philosophy which was then active in bold conspiracy.

" Likest to thee in shape and count'nance bright,
" Then shining heav'nly fair, a goddess arm'd
" Out of thy head I sprung : amazement seiz'd
" All th' host of heav'n—Back they recoil'd, afraid
" At first, and call'd me Sin."

The doctrine alluded to is a fundamental principle of jacobinism. It has been variously described by those who were unacquainted with its nature, and by those who wished to conceal its innate horror

* Mercure Hist. et Pol: Octobre 1791. Pastoret, dans la Séance de l'Assemblée Nat. 25 Octobre. The whole assembly despised the pretensions of wealth and hereditary distinction, and pretended to associate in their filthy idolatry " the powers " of talent, and vertu."

and deformity by wilful misrepresentation; but the essential maxim, without any complexity of phrase, is that "it is lawful to pursue a political advantage by means of actual crime."

This doctrine was not confined to that certainty of beneficial result which, in practice, will too often mislead the judgment of the sincerest lovers of truth and virtue. In ordinary cases, we are too apt to think it not unlawful to do a little evil that great and certain good may come of it; a far more fatal error was that proclaimed and carried into complete effect by the moralists of France. They were satisfied to do the greatest positive evil for an end considered good only by themselves, and deprecated by virtuous minds; and even that end not to be certainly attained, but only resting in probable and even distant contingency. By these means the private and the public judgment was liberated from rule and precedent, and raised to a function of conclusively determining the nature and result of its own decisions. That determination might be made in the heat of vengeance, the deception of error, the thirst of emolument, the perversion of selfishness, or under the influence of any other passion which convulses the mind or darkens the understanding. The intention and the motive of any action being an end of great contingent advantage, that was abundantly sufficient, and whatever apparent or necessary evil might be involved in its natural or immediate consequences, it was adjudged to be lawful and meritorious.

In the political convulsions of preceding ages, whether the struggle was on a question of succession, or for the establishment of one form of government in preference to another; a revolution being effectuated, or a rebellion being terminated, there was an end to the rancour and evil tendency of such contention. Whatever crimes had been perpetrated in the course of civil warfare, the brazen tablets of the moral code were left by both parties unmutilated and unimpaired. Respect to religious principle was invariably kept inviolate. The fury of the storm having subsided, the usual tranquillity of nature was restored; and in that tranquillity the gentle affections of the heart and the amiable restraints of moral discipline were resumed by a people whom the calamities of domestic discord had not corrupted.

But it was otherwise of necessity in the proceedings of the French revolution. The torrent was impetuous, and became deeper and more tempestuous in its destructive course; but it has never deviated from its own peculiar law: it has displayed no phenomenon of nature, except that of its original existence. A revolution begun by an immense population united in the same pernicious sentiment, unfettered and uncontrouled, endued with sovereign authority, liberated from all restraint of justice and compunction, taught that crimes were the lawful implements of its power, and that no institution, civil or religious, was independent of its will, organized by law in permanent insurrection; such a revolution naturally proceeded in the manner which history relates. After the first usurpation of the aristocracy of talents, it was natural that the people should be capricious in loyalty to their original literary leaders. Ambition not being confined to the compilers of dictionaries of science and literary journals, of philosophical treatises and of moral disquisitions, it was natural that another set of men who had still greater facilities of obtaining popular support, should succeed to the power and influence of that aristocracy.

It was natural that the publishers of newspapers and of weekly registers, the fabricators of calumny and falshood in the shape of useful intelligence, the calculators of almanacs, the writers of pamphlets, the orators of debating clubs, the managers of petty parochial litigation, the sturdy defenders of opinion at ale-houses, and in the public squares, and all the presumptuous intriguing candidates for low municipal function, should in due time assert their claim to the succession of the sovereignty; and that the multitude, more assiduously courted by these latter demagogues, with whom they could fraternize in more perfect assimilation, should withdraw their favor from the great original aristocracy.

The literary faction was finally triumphant in France on the ever-memorable days of the tenth of August and the second of September, 1792. They could not tolerate the name of royalty, though the whole power of the state was vested in their hands as the leaders of a factious democratic national assembly, while the civic crown rested without independent function or respect on the brow of a patient unresisting prince, whose injuries proceeded from the submissive mildness and the beneficence of his heart, and whose virtues will be recorded among the misfortunes of this disastrous age.

The early and incurable fault of that monarch, a quality at first commended with high eulogium, and afterwards discredited by an ungrateful people, was a confidence in the professions of the men of letters and philosophers, with a great desire to ameliorate the condition of his subjects, upon their principles of reformation rather than by the exercise of his legitimate hereditary prerogative.— Thence it was that the first measures of his government were the pardon and recal of the Duc de

Choiseul and the factious members of the parliament, whom his predecessor had punished with exile for first promulging, in bold remonstrance, the doctrines of the rights of man and of resistance to authority. The storm of rebellion would have been raised by those men but for the firm loyalty of the chancellor Maupeou; by whose counsel Louis XV. had adopted measures of rigour and asserted the rights of his crown.

The youthful sovereign was not guided by the sage precepts left for his instruction by his father the Dauphin, who met with premature death in 1765. That enlightened prince, at that early period, had ascertained the principles of the philosophers, and the dangers which their influence occasioned. "I have studied them," said he; "I have examined
" their principles and their consequences. In some
" I have discovered a spirit of libertinism and cor-
" ruption, interested in decrying that morality
" which imposes a restraint on their efforts; and
" in casting doubts on the existence of a future
" state, the apprehension of which fills them with
" alarm: others, led away by the ridiculous vanity
" of erecting a system of their own, seek to reduce
" the Deity to a level with their own understand-
" ing, and to reason on his attributes and his mys-
" teries, in the same manner as it is permitted to
" reason on his works. They maintain that the
" throne was the work of violence, and that what
" was raised by force may by force be pulled down
" and destroyed; that the people can only lend,
" not cede, their authority, which they have a right
" to delegate and to recal, as personal interest,
" their sole master, requires. What our passions
" would barely insinuate, our philosophers openly
" teach; that a prince may do whatever he can,
" and that he has discharged his duty when he has

" satisfied his desires; for, in truth, if this law of
" interest, that is to say, of the caprice of human
" passions, should be generally adopted, so as to
" cause the law of God to be forgotten, then all
" ideas of justice and injustice, virtue and vice,
" moral good and evil, would be effaced and anni-
" hilated in the human mind; thrones would tot-
" ter; subjects would become factious and intract-
" able; sovereigns would lose their benevolence
" and humanity; the people would be always in a
" state of revolt or a state of oppression."*

Louis XVI. regardless of that precept, called to his council the known patrons and confederates of that pernicious sect. He checked the zeal of the archbishop of Paris and the clergy to controul their machinations. He gave establishment to the principles of rebellion in America, by the aid he afforded to the revolted colonies; he allowed free scope to seditious inquiry, by the various projects of reform which he recommended to his assemblies of the notables; while he promoted the hopes and facilitated the means of conspiracy, by the confidence which he reposed in Turgot, Necker, and Calonne, who were at once the administrators and the betrayers of his power.

Immediately after the commencement of the commotions he yielded the dignity of his crown and the rights of his prerogative to the mercy of a tumultuous usurping democracy. He rejected the assistance of those who would have died in his cause, and at the instigation of traiterous counsellors he contributed by his proclamations to debauch the fidelity of his troops. He permitted his illustrious relations and the natural supporters of his authority to be vilified, robbed, degraded, and

* Vie de Dauphin's Pere de Louis XVI. par L'Abbe Proyart. Pages 74 et 75.

driven into exile. He renounced the hereditary title of his monarchy, and consented, by a new denomination, to accept a powerless sceptre from the hands of traitors and assassins. To that execrable faction acting in the name of the new philosophy, he sacrificed his family, his clergy, his nobility, his magistracy, and all orders of privilege and antient institution. He was content to become an impotent pageant of royalty, the mockery of his unprincipled enemies, and the tool of irreconcileable conspirators against every species of lawful authority, when he announced to all the world, by a letter under his own hand, that he had voluntarily accepted the constitution of 1791.

To all the subsequent commands and solicitations of the inveterate foe, he was equally compliant. He gave his assent to the declaration of war against those sovereigns who allied to restore him to liberty and power. To every vindictive measure against the princes of his house, and the loyal emigrants who were armed in his defence, he gave the sanction of his name; and finally, at the consummation of treason in the unprovoked rebellion of the tenth of August, he put himself and his family in the power of the conspirators, and became a prisoner of the National Assembly.

The character of Louis XVI. is sanctified by his misfortunes. His errors, alike fatal to himself and to his people, were such as a generous mind will not now severely censure. Incapable of deception or evil design, he had confided in the sincerity of those who professed themselves the friends of truth and virtue, and the supporters of the rights and duties of mankind. His mind, endued with gentleness and unbounded humanity, was incapable of that hardihood and vigour by which alone he could counteract the perils which surrounded him. Rather than that one human being should suffer in his cause, he submitted to the loss of power, of reputation, and of life, and by his unwise forbearance, inspired with courage the aspiring propagators of that new doctrine which attacked the foundations of his government, and at last was sealed by his blood. Our children, while they lament the weakness of his judgment, must revere the mildness, patience, fortitude, and pious resignation with which he endured the rage of persecution and all his unequalled calamities. When their indignant tears shall flow at the recital of his last sufferings, they will honour him as a martyr in the cause of order and religion, and that mercy with which he forgave the guilt of his relentless murderers, will cast into temporary oblivion whatever evil effect has resulted and shall result to mankind from the amiable and benignant qualities of his heart.

Had there been any sense of gratitude in the minds of his enemies, they would not have immolated a prince, to whose virtues they were indebted for the power which they so flagrantly abused. But the spirit of jacobinism is startled at no enormity of crime, and never feels remorse. It was enough to excite their hatred, that Louis had the title of a King, and that, by his destruction, they might hope to enjoy all the powers of sovereignty. They proceeded by calumny, by avowed sedition, and by a massacre, of which the cruelty surpasses whatever is related of savages in their wildest excesses, to overthrow his throne, and to declare the establishment of a republic. At the first sitting of the convention, royalty was for ever abolished in France, and the republic, one and indivisible, was proclaimed.

Then the philosophers imagined that their triumph was complete. In the legislative body, their influence was without limit. The executive power was wholly confided to their hands. The convention was opened with an adulatory harangue from Manuel, who boasted that in addressing that representation of the people, he stood before an assembly of philosophers, whose occupation it would be to labour for the welfare of the world. " Il voyoit dans la réunion des repre-" sentans du peuple, une assemblée de philosophes " occupés à preparer le bonheur du monde."*

But the oligarchy of the men of letters discovered too late, that a people habituated to principles of insurrection will fluctuate in opinion, and that their change of favor is destructive. " Rerum potiri volunt. Honores quos quietâ re-" publicâ desperant, perturbatâ, consequi se posse " arbitrantur." But those honors, when they had attained them, could not be permanent. They wished to deny the affiliation of that fearful democracy and its legitimate issue, the infuriated phantom of jacobinism, which, like the Satanic offspring, began to torment and threaten its natural sire, " with pangs unfelt before."

" I know thee not, nor ever saw till now,
" Sight more detestable than him and thee."

Their horror and unnatural abandonment of the unquestionable lineage were vain. In vain did Brissot and the philosophical conspirators complain of " laws without execution, constituted " authorities impotent or disgraced, crimes unpu-" nished, property attacked, personal safety vio-" lated, the morals of the people corrupted, no " constitution, no government, no justice: all " which are the true features of anarchy."† These were the crimes by which the men of letters had advanced themselves to power. They had hoped

* Journal Historique et Politique. 17 September. 1792.

to " ride in the whirlwind and direct the storm." But another party, upon their own principles and with equal rights, wrested from them their implements of revolutionary agency, and they fell detested and unpitied.

The abstract principle, now commended by the Edinburgh Reviewers, is identical with that which was then asserted by the prevailing faction in France, when " the bulk, the mass of the " people, nay, the very odious many headed beast, " the multitude, the mob itself, in despite of the " higher classes, and in direct opposition to them, " raised up the standard of insurrection, and bore " it through massacre, and through victory." Experience was, at that time, feeble to guide the judgment upon this new principle of rebellion. Civilized society had been often convulsed, tyranny had been resisted and subdued by insurrection, and the condition of mankind had been ameliorated by prudent and just resistance to lawless oppression. Such an example was afforded in our own history at the ever-memorable establishment of King William and Queen Mary upon our imperial throne. But never before was there a national attempt to give to the multitude, at large, a right to cashier their governors, and to change their government at will.

Modern history affords but two instances, which can be interpreted as precedents of that case. It was the insurrection of the Anabaptists in Germany, in the early part of the sixteenth century, and the rebellion of the English colonies of America.

In the great contest between the Roman Catholics and the Reformers, in consequence of the rapid diffusion of the new tenets, the most inveterate hatred and jealousy reigned between the two parties, and with the antipathy natural to religious disputes, each suspected the hostile intentions of the other. Perhaps this mutual distrust was on neither side without foundation; but the Catholics, in particular, were justly alarmed with the application to secular affairs of the new principles in regard to religion. Men of ardent imaginations and licentious characters indulged themselves in the wildest speculations, and committed the most abominable disorders. Muncer and Store, originally disciples of Luther, became the chiefs of the sect of Anabaptists; they arrogated the gift of prophecy, formed a kingdom of the elect on earth, introduced a community of goods and wives, abjured all civil, as well as religious authority, and threw off all restraints, divine and human. The emissaries of these fanatics spread among the peasants, and found little difficulty in rousing against the nobles, magistrates, and clergy, a class of men, who groaned under all the oppressions of feudal despotism. (1524.) Rebellions at once broke out, as if by concert, in almost every part of Germany. The peasants took the field in numerous bodies, and giving full scope to the sentiments of vengeance which they had long suppressed, spared neither sex nor age, and rendered the provinces, which they over-run, a dreadful scene of devastation and carnage. But the sovereigns of both parties, uniting to crush a rebellion, which equally affected the rights and safety of all, the sect of Anabaptists was broken and dispersed. Muncer, their chief, received on the scaffold the reward of his crimes; and the peasants were reduced to obedience, after no less than 100,000 had fallen in various encounters.*

* This account is extracted from Coxe's House of Austria, 1st vol.

That antisocial rebellion founded in fanaticism, and applied to secular affairs, was not to effectuate a scheme of Atheism and general immorality, but to establish what was believed to be a triumph of religion, and the dominion of the saints, and had little resemblance in motive, or in object, to the modern revolution: if it had any such resemblance, its early application to the new crisis might have been beneficial, as a warning and an example; as a warning to the leaders of insurrection, to divert them from prosecuting their execrable designs; as an example to all sovereigns to suspend all partial differences, and instantly to unite with all their forces for the suppression of so dangerous a commotion.

The principle of rebellion, adopted by the United States of America, had no resemblance whatsoever to the doctrine then triumphant in France, and now asserted in this country. That revolution was attempted to be justified by the alleged tyranny of the English government. It was preceded originally by complaint and petition in language sufficiently decorous; nor did it assume the character of national resistance to authority, till every expedient of prayer and of remonstrance had been ineffectually tried. At last, the declaration of independence, which they made the foundation of the constitutional law then adopted, was published by congress. That instrument contained a long enumeration of grievances, which, if they had been true, would have amounted to an abdication of the government, such as they asserted to have taken place; of those grievances there was no hope of redress, and the emancipation would have been justifiable by the necessity of the case. But in that proceeding there was little appearance of popular sedition. In the congress was found all that part of the American nation, which was capable of sound deliberation, of exercising judgment, and acting with such discretion as is necessary to legalize any national act, and to express the public will. The ancient constitutional assemblies of the provinces, the property and influence of the great commercial towns, and the weight of the liberal professions were present in adequate representation; but there was no claim asserted in favour of the great mass of the community, nor was it assumed by that enlightened body, that their separation from the British empire could rest upon any other basis than that of oppressive and hopeless grievance, and absolute necessity. The federal government, then provided, was to be permanently independent of popular will, and to be of perpetual force in the United States of America.*

Such was not the prevailing dogma of the French revolution. By the abstract principle of that proceeding, neither dignity of station, opulence, hereditary or acquired, the merit of past service, or the validity of local reputation were allowed to confer any national privilege or preeminence; but the unalienable power of sovereignty was held to appertain to the vilest and the most elevated, to the most wretched and the most opulent, to the most ignorant and the most enlightened, to the basest and the most virtuous members of society, with equal title, and in equal participation.

Though experience was almost silent as to the effective operation of such a maxim of anarchy and

---

* The reader may consult the declaration, by the representatives of the United States of America, in general congress assembled, 4th July, 1776, in which the correctness of the above statement will appear.

disorder, yet that which did immediately ensue might have been anticipated by the common sagacity of an incorrupted mind. The people, at large, in every possible condition of society, called to the exercise of power, must be impelled by passion, and cannot be guided by reason. They cannot deliberate, nor can they foresee and regulate those numberless contingencies of human affairs, upon the least of which the welfare of the state, and the happiness of its subjects, must daily and hourly depend. In their council, wisdom may be silenced and dishonoured, while

—" the rattling tongue
" of saucy and audacious eloquence"

is heard with rapturous applause. By their justice, the virtue of an Asistides may be punished with ostracism, and the parasites and retainers of a Philip be supported and commended. In the little republic of Geneva, there was once an instance of prudence and moderation in such an assembly. There was a law which provided that, at the end of every five years, a convention of the people should be held with sovereign power. That convention met but once, (1712) and then it afforded a remarkable proof of the virtue and good sense which sometimes influenced the public judgment, before philosophy had raised its standard. Its first and only resolution was, that it should meet no more. Unhappily the example of that democracy is solitary. All other democracies have been found as ambitious as they were restless and unwise. In the natural world, disorder and ruin must instantly ensue, but for the provident care of that presiding intelligence which constituted and maintains the universal harmony and dependence. So, in our political constitutions, if the combining principle of a superior power be withdrawn, and the various orders liberated from the controul of superintending wisdom, and cast into elemental strife, a wild and fatal uproar must succeed. Whether the disorganizing dogma be promulged by a Catiline from personal depravity, by a Muncer, and a Storc, from religious enthusiasm, or by men of letters and philosophers, from a more dangerous vanity and ambition, the same destructive results must inevitably follow.

The Edinburgh Reviewers would, nevertheless, encourage the trial of an additional experiment. They promise that " the example of one revolu-" tion will prevent a repetition of its enormities in " the progress of the other."* The French philosophers were equally liberal in promise, and confident in hope. It is better to trust to experience and the reason of things, than to be guided by that counsel of the Edinburgh Reviewers.

It was natural, and seems to be a sort of retributive justice, that the learned aristocracy of France should expiate its guilt and presumption by that same instrument of death, which they had employed in the indiscriminate slaughter of the innocent and loyal. It was natural that the excess of turpitude, cruelty, and oppression, should rage during many successive years in the triumph of the various factions which successively prevailed. After a long duration of anarchy and terror, it was natural that the people, weary of their own fatal pretences to a sovereignty, which they could not exercise, should feel just resentment towards all its bold asserters. That they should finally abandon the revolutionary principle, and submit to the rule of some triumph-

* Page 223.

ant warrior, who should consolidate in his own title all the claims of philosophy, and perpetuate the abominable doctrines of jacobin morality, by making it the basis of his public law.

The whole military force of France, without hesitation, at his command abandoned the republican institutions. The men of letters had forgotten the lessons of history, and the example of Cromwell, in the preceding century. Armies must have a military chief, and are never faithful to democratic command. The National Assembly had shewn little sagacity in their notion of the soldiers of liberty, and in their institution of the national troops, and of the municipal guards. Mirabeau did not exercise his usual foresight and penetration, when he demanded in a tone of triumph and of defiance, " et que sont " ces troupes si non les Troupes de la Liberté ? " pourquoi les avons nous instituées si elles ne sont " pas eternellement destinées a conserver ce qu'elles " ont conquis ?" His unsoldier-like, motley, undisciplined hordes of insurgents were at that time animated with the ardor of insurrection, and with democratic zeal; but they were no sooner converted, by the necessities of war, into a true and well-disciplined militia, than they became conscious of the dignity and power of arms. They acquired contempt for the turbulent, tyrannizing municipalities of manufacturers and artificers, which sometimes affected to be their masters, and sometimes courted them to confederate in their plans of sedition. They rather adhered to the order of military nature. The glory of a triumphant liberal leader, who knew better how to touch the springs of their affection, and promised to gratify them with substantial reward, they naturally preferred to the insolent pretensions of a vulgar democracy, whose unsubstantial thanks, given with jealousy and mistrust, were the only recompense in their means to bestow.*

The French revolution which was planned by the men of letters, a hundred years ago, that the emancipated nations might be under their guidance and controul; the principles of which, during all the intervening period, they insidiously and laboriously inculcated in books of science and of amusement, in the schools, and upon the stage, and by whatever other means, and wherever else opinion might be influenced, till at last the public mind was contaminated throughout from the throne of the monarch to the

---

* The prophetic wisdom of that prodigy of our nature, Mr. Burke, distinctly anticipated this termination of the revolution.

" It is known that armies have hitherto yielded a very precarious and uncertain obedience to any senate or popular authority; and they will, least of all, yield it to an assembly, which is to have only the continuance of two years. The officers must totally lose the characteristic disposition of military men, if they see with perfect submission, and due admiration, the dominion of pleaders; especially when they find, that they have a new court to pay to an endless succession of those pleaders, whose military policy, and the genius of whose command (if they should have any) must be as uncertain as their duration is transient. In the weakness of one kind of authority, and in the fluctuation of all, the officers of an army will remain, for some time, mutinous and full of faction, until some popular general, who understands the art of conciliating the soldiery, and who possesses a true spirit of command, shall draw the eyes of all men upon himself. Armies will obey him on his personal account. There is no other way of securing military obedience in this state of things. But the moment in which that event shall happen, the person, who really commands the army, is your master; the master (that is little) of your king, the master of your assembly, the master of your whole republic."

See that immortal publication, his Reflections upon the French Revolution. Page 390, of the last octavo edition.

peasant's cottage; that revolution, which at last broke out in the form of a supreme National Assembly for the correction of abuses and the regenerating the state, has terminated, as was predicted, and as it inevitably must terminate, in the establishment of a military tyranny, the most absolute that ever enchained mankind. The moral doctrine of jacobinism is triumphant in the person of the most unrelenting conqueror that ever desolated the earth.

In the histories of those warriors, who were able to subdue all Europe by the terror of their arms, we are taught that the atrocities, which they committed in their career of victory, are palliated, in degree, by the barbarism of the ages in which they flourished. Ferocious as they were, their ravages and cruelties were committed in the tumult of battles, and upon those whom they had attacked in open and declared hostility. When the capital of the Christian world was taken and sacked, by the Gothic Alaric, he encouraged his troops boldly to seize the rewards of their valour, and to enrich themselves with the spoils of a wealthy and effeminate people. But he exhorted them to spare the lives of the unresisting citizens, and to respect the churches of the apostles as holy and inviolable sanctuaries. * The savage mind of the Scythian Attila was not inaccessible to pity. His suppliant enemies might confide in his assurance of peace or pardon; and he was considered by his subjects, as a just and indulgent master. He delighted in war, but he founded his vast monarchy on the basis of popular superstition, which, however offensive it might be to the sceptics of this enlightened age, is far pre-

* V. Gibbon's Decline and Fall. Ch

ferable to that impiety which gives force and permanence to all our malignant passions. *

Napoleon, of humble station and obscure origin, was born at Ajacio, in a little dependency of the French crown. He received his subsistence and education from the noble beneficence of the king of France, and was an elève of that unfortunate monarch in his military school at Brienne, at the commencement of the revolution. His heart was never warmed by the sense of gratitude towards any benefactor. He very early forgot the benefit which he had received in his youth, and entered into the service of those who had murdered his patron and abolished royalty. He became a soldier of the republic, and took an oath of allegiance to the sovereignty of the nation.

His mind, astute in project and daring in execution, was fitted for revolutionary warfare. He was distinguished at the siege of Toulon, and acquired the favour of Barras, by whom he was promoted to the rank of a general. Under the command of that representative, he headed the troops which massacred the inhabitants of Paris, and established the memorable revolution of the fourth and fift of October, 1795, when the constitution of the third year was enacted, to which he took an oath of fidelity.

The revolution of the fourth of September, 1797, by which that constitution was violated and destroyed, the Directory were enabled to effectuate by his concurrence, counsel, and promise of support. In an address to his army in Italy, where he then commanded, he had just said, " let us " swear, fellow soldiers, by the manes of the pa. " triots who have died by our side, eternal hatred

―――――――――――
* V. Gibbon Dec. ne and Fall. Chap. xxxiv.

" to the enemies of the constitution of the third
" year."

The details of his Italian campaigns are worthy of being recorded, as they will be, in a less perishable work. Here it is sufficient to observe, that history does not unfold any system of warfare, in any age, more detestable for cruelty, extortion, and pillage, than that which established his fame, and led to his gigantic grandeur. The great principle of that warfare was to excite the passions of the lower classes against their governors and superiors. It was a continual appeal to the prevalent immorality of the age, and was successfully made " to procure the solemn acknowledgement
" of the rights of nations, and to change the form
" of every government."*

In that campaign, among numberless other acts of unprecedented violence, it may be remembered, that, in the excess of unprovoked fury, he directed the indiscriminate massacre of eight hundred of the inhabitants of the town of Benasco, which he rased from its foundations, and delivered the whole country on the borders of the Mincio to the plunder of his ferocious soldiery. In every state the churches and religious institutions were pillaged by his army, without distinction. Every fund consecrated by ancient piety to charitable uses, he fearlessly confiscated. He seized every public treasure; he subjected every village to rapine and robbery; the sacred priesthood, and all the forms of public worship he derided, insulted and abolished; the temples and the holy mysteries he mutilated and profaned; and by a proclamation made in his own name, he ordered the troops to shoot whoever had not taken an oath of obedience to

* Redacteur Official. 30 June, 1797.

his authority, and to burn every place where the tocsin should be sounded, and to put its inhabitants to death.

The overthrow of the papacy, brought about by intrigues, in direct violation of the solemn assurances of friendship, and actually subsisting treaty, was accompanied with a savage disdain of the venerable character of the aged pontiff, whose piety and virtues would have adorned a purer profession of christianity; and was a new evidence that the adventurous soldier had adopted all the principles of the revolution, and that sanctity of life, integrity of heart, and the decrepitude of years, made sacred by wisdom and benevolence, were naturally the contempt and hatred of the illuminated advocate of the new morality.

The expedition, to wrest from the Ottoman dominion, with whom the republic was in profound peace, Egypt, its richest dependency, and thereby to gratify the ambition and mark the contempt of treaties which distinguished the counsels of the Directory, was his peculiar project. Then it was that he openly renounced the sect of Christianity, and proclaimed "that he venerated more than the " Mamlues, God his prophet and the Koran."*

His warfare in Egypt, as it is recorded by Denon, an authentic narrator, under his immediate direction, from his own imperial press, abounded with acts of deliberate murder, violence, and pillage, which no history whatsoever can parallel. Upon landing at Alexandria " he put all his adversaries " to death at the breach." " His soldiers, heated " by wine and by the climate, inspired so much " terror among the lower classes, that they kept " their females in concealment." (page-60, vol. i.)

Such was their wanton oppression, that "the timid "Egyptians soon began to regret their former "tyrants." (page 335.) To crush resistance "a "great carnage of the rebels was made by General "Dumas." "Under the pretence of seeking for "provisions, the brutal soldiery sought the grati- "fications of their impetuous lust, and for want of "being able to explain their object, and to make "themselves understood, they killed the furious "natives." (Vol. ii. Page 12.) "They put to "the sword a thousand of the deluded natives, "who pursued their march to give them the im- "pression of their being vindictive, and to con- "vince them that they should punish severely "those who were disposed to doubt that all they "did was finally for their own good." (Page 37.) "If the poor inhabitants did not express that "doubt, but supplied the wants of the army, they "saw their provisions eaten with regularity, and "might come in for their portion of them, pre- "serving a part of their dwellings from being "burnt, and but a few of their wives and daugh- "ters were ravished." (Page 46.) Let it be re- membered that these atrocities were perpetrated under Bonaparte, in a country with which he was not at war, with the pretence of friendly regene- ration, to carry on the great work of the revolu- tion; and were sanctioned by the counsel of an aristocracy of talents which accompanied him in that expedition!*

The massacre of three thousand eight hundred Turkish prisoners, at Jaffa, and the poisoning of five hundred and eighty of his own diseased sol-

* These extracts, from Denon's Travels in Egypt, during the campaign of General Bonaparte, are the same which are quoted from Dr. Aikin's translation, in the account of that work given in the first volume of the Edinburgh Review.

diers, at the same place, as related by Sir Robert Wilson, are not instances of greater atrocity than those which, in his magnanimity, or his contempt of virtuous reputation, he permitted his own historian to relate, with all the ostentation and embellishment of a national work.

These were the heroic actions on which the great Napoleon founded his early reputation for arts, policy, and military prowess. By the fame which he had thus acquired, he was enabled at length to overthrow that government of which he was at the last moment the sworn supporter, and to the glory of which he had dedicated the splendor of his success and the fruits of all his labors. In a barbarous age, the nations which yielded to Alaric and to Attila were already familiar with the excesses of their savage conqueror; but the excesses of all other conquerors were mild, moderate, and conciliating, compared with the systematic proceedings of Bonaparte, in an age the most distinguished for civilization, learning, manners, and humanity. Those proceedings are not the less atrocious for being accompanied by a declared infidelity to the compacts of society, on which alone the security of nations can rest, and by an open abandonment of all religious institution, on which alone the hopes and the happiness of individuals can find stability.

Enabled to crush the constitution, and to assume the exercise of the supreme power, he still maintained his duplicity and contempt of moral obligation. In the Council of the Ancients, on the 8th of November, 1799, he exclaimed in the presence of two of the Directory, " we demand a re-" public founded on the principles of liberty, equa-" lity, and national representation." At that instant the republic was sinking into annihilation with all the host of assassins, libellers, and traitors, who in its name had tortured mankind. The destructive phantom of the liberty, equality, and national representation of the reforming patriots of the insurrection against Louis XVI. having completed his part in the drama, and blasted all the expectations of such as imagined he had any act of goodness to perform, was then about to quit the stage for ever, and to give place to triumphant despotism. On the following day, Bonaparte having completed his military preparations, gave the Assembly to understand, that, " the God of war, " and his good fortune would protect him." Then Murat, since promoted to kingly honor, dispersed the legislative body, and with the bayonet drove the members through all the avenues of their hall. A remnant of that body, the same night, decreed that the directory had ceased to exist, and created the provisional power of the consulate.

Whatever was most guilty and pernicious in the spirit of jacobinism; whatever principles of disloyalty, rebellion, treachery, perjury, and usurpation, had marked the progress of the revolution from its earliest commencement to this its natural termination, appeared as a distinctive feature of the consulate of Bonaparte. Had the French nation, torn by faction, desolated by crime, weary of the tumultuous tyranny of crafty atheistical regicides, and impelled by remorse; had it begun to mourn its miseries with penitence, and to sympathize with the suffering nations which were depressed by that relentless tyranny; in such a state of mind had it passed under the rule of a bold and resolute master, whose stern power should have awed factious conspirators, and whose severe but just administration should have repressed an habitual fondness of his people for rapine, slaughter, and disorder; then there might have been some hope that such vigorous despotism would have some respect to public law; that the sense and the restraints of piety and justice might be restored eventually to the embruted multitude; and that in the process of moral amelioration, a time might come when France would resume her station in civilized society, when her greatness might be compatible with the safety of other nations, and when her people would join to lament and to repair the ruin and devastation which had been perpetrated by a savage democracy.

But in the consular power of Bonaparte, and in the imperial rule of the great Napoleon, are still perceived the lineaments of pure, unadulterated jacobinism. In an elaborate work, by Hauterive, who was his foreign minister, ("Chef de Relations "exterieurs") published by his authority, immediately after his accession to the consular dignity, it was distinctly announced to all the world, that the federative system which he adopted was that same upon which all the preceding revolutionary authorities had acted. It was founded in the same disregard of treaties and public law, the same principles of universal insurrection, the same means of robbery, plunder, and confiscation, the same maxim of appealing to the people in all countries against the authority of their legitimate sovereigns. "If " France cannot otherwise extend the relations of " her continental federative system, she will em- " ploy the only means which the folly of the states " that have abandoned her alliance, and the obsti- " nacy of those which persist in a sanguinary war, " have left at her disposal. For federative sub- " sidies, she will substitute military subsidies; and " if princes disregard the voice of self interest, " which dictates an alliance, she will virtually ally " hers

" pable of defending, and will convert into auxi-
" liaries all the means of subsistence, and of de-
" fence that can by any ways be furnished by the
" territory which her armies may occupy."

How successfully the tyrant has proceeded upon his grand federative maxim of jacobinism, it would be painful, and is not necessary to detail. Let that task devolve upon the future historian, whose narrative will not excite the horror and the virtuous hatred which must accompany our present observation, and our interest in the result of those aweful events. It suffices here to call to mind the mission of Sebastiani, during the short period of tranquillity which followed the treaties of Luneville and Amiens, instituted to continue the project of the Egyptian expedition, and to revolutionize Greece and the islands of the Archipelago! Then the enslaving of the republics of the Helvetic confederacy! Then the establishment of Louis and Joseph Bonaparte upon the thrones of Holland and Naples! Then the assuming of the iron crown of Lombardy! Then the establishment of Jerom, the fugitive from America, in the new formed kingdom of Westphalia! Then the depositions and new creations of the submissive princes who did rule, and of the more submissive upstarts who now rule in the states of the Confederation of the Rhine, which followed the dissolution of the ancient Germanic empire! Then the attempt to prevent all possible recurrence to the ancient law of Europe, by the perpetual exclusion of England from the councils of princes! Then the project of changing the old maritime law and system of neutrality for our more effectual destruction! And, lastly, that act of usurpation, the perfidy and atrocity of which no former act had equalled, the degradation and imprisonment of the royal family of Spain, and the inauguration of Joseph upon their throne.

As concise may be the allusion to the moral qualities of Jacobinism still triumphant in the practice of the imperial government. Such was the treacherous murder of Toussaint, the possession of whose person was obtained by a solemn pledge and assurance of safety and protection! Then the execrated seizure of the Duke D'Enghien; that distinguished member of his illustrious house, and the hope of all the remnant of the antient honor of France, in a neutral territory, by a furious banditti in the silence of the night; taken from his rest, the last which he was ever to enjoy, while unconscious of danger, and unsuspicious of attack; hurried to the capital of his great enemy; brought without a moment's repose before a ferocious military inquisition; his person being identified, doomed to immediate death, and that doom instantly executed by a band of Italian mercenaries! his persecutor denied him the last consolation of our mortal nature;

"Cut off even in the blossoms of his sin :
"Unhouzzled, disappointed, unanneal'd;
"No reckoning made, but sent to his account
"With all his imperfections on his head!

Then the judicial execution of the pauper, Palm, of too mean condition for imperial vengeance, but murdered in a foreign state, to shew to all the world, that the thoughts of men must be bound by his tyranny, and that the lowest of mankind must suffer for presuming to proclaim the truth, or to assert the freedom of the press; (our own peculiar boast, secured by the sacred safeguard of our laws!) Lastly, the recent transactions of the Spani

English soldiers in cold blood, triumphantly announced in the imperial bulletin, and published in the gazette of France! the burning of the town of Benevente, and the massacre of its inhabitants! and the rest of the atrocious actions which make up the long catalogue of crimes, in that violation of the rights of an independent sovereign.

If the French revolution had been originally and essentially political, and had been welcomed into being by its enthusiastic admirers, as an instrumental means of diffusing universally the principles of any species of republican institution, it is hardly possible that the outrage with which it commenced and proceeded should have been tolerated and applauded by those who profess themselves the advocates of general liberty. In that case it is incredible, that those whose literary labours prepared the public mind for the vast convulsion, should have long basked in the sunshine of royal favour, and that even kings should have become their disciples, and have zealously contributed to their success. The heads of the antient monarchies would have shewn an earlier and more resolute resistance to a licentious democracy, and would have waited till the last extremity of subjugation, before they would have acknowledged its principles of rebellion, and have sent their envoys in flattering submission to confederate and fraternize with such a species of sovereignty. We can hardly be persuaded that there would have existed a party in all countries, which should invariably have opposed itself to whatever was hostile to France, and have made an outcry for peace at every period of the revolutionary war. Those men shewed little indignation at the violation of property, the degradation and extirpation of rank the robbery and assassination of the ministers of religion: they witnessed without any expression of alarm the proclamation of atheism, and the abandonment of all established morality in public transactions or in private life: they were not appalled at the overthrow of thrones, and the subjugation of powerful commonwealths, nor at the methods of treachery and rapine, by which the dominion of France was extended on every side: they did not censure the institutions of anarchy and licentiousness, which followed the martyrdom of Louis XVI; nor were they less favourable to the ministration of the Committee of Public Safety established in the capital, to overawe the National Convention itself, and of its dependant committees of surveillance organized throughout the republic, to make the reign of terror universal.* They never exulted in any interruption of the victorious career with which the revolutionary banner was borne by the triumphant armies; nor did they reprobate the violence of the conscription, nor the oppression of the taxation, which recruited and paid these prodigious establishments. If the question was fundamentally political, could the tyranny of Roberspierre be reconciled to republican zeal? or were the insolent domination and gaudy decorations of the five directors consistent with the simplicity of a democratic contitution? We must search deeper than political sentiment, to unravel the mystery of that unvaried applause, which all the actors of the interesting drama have obtained in succession, and to account for that uniform ap-

---

* The expence of these establishments, and of the revolutionary tribunals, which judged the unfortunate persons doomed to die by these Committees, was not less than thirty two m

probation which has been bestowed upon the apparent inconsistencies of the plot.

If the revolution was purely of a moral quality, if it originated in a great conspiracy to establish a domination of the aristocracy of talents by the destruction of all religion and all moral obligation, then those who adopted the principles and participate in the ambition of that aristocracy, might without inconsistency applaud the early outrages of the multitude, when they were instigated by Bailly and La Fayette, to demand a constitution ornamented with a shadow of degraded loyalty, but completed upon the foundation of the imputed Rights of Man; they might equally applaud their massacres and thirst for judicial slaughter, when guided entirely by the philosophers, by Roland, Brissot and Pétion, they asserted the dogmas of natural equality, and framed a republican form of government. Their approbation would not fail when the same multitude roused to greater energy by Roberspierre, Danton, and Marat, claimed the unalienable exercise of power, and declared themselves in permanent insurrection. That uninterrupted fervor of the great proceeding, in all its tragical and tumultuous progress, was natural to those, whose hatred to the establishments of christianity is paramount to all other considerations; who regard no weariness or calamity, in their labor to exalt a shapeless infidelity as a triumphant national profession; and apply the utmost force of depraved yet powerful intellect, to break through the restraints of morals, and to be liberated from the bondage of conscience, justice, and ancient law. The scheme is still progressive; and whatsoever other scenes and changes are to come, as yet involved in "shadows, clouds, and darkness," the same commendation and contempt of all its horrors, will be afforded by its cold-blooded speculative admirers. The past transactions were almost necessary to its successful course, and must not therefore be severely scrutinized by those who think that "it is lawful to pursue a moral and "political advantage by means of actual crime." It is that principle alone which gave toleration to the excesses of the extinct democracy, and can now reconcile any man to the threatening tyranny of the power subsisting in France.

Among all the conquerors who have desolated the earth in the revolutions of empires, Napoleon has a peculiar character and fortune. Alexander was the hereditary possessor of a state, which had already been distinguished for vigour and prudence. He triumphed over the nations sunk in slothful effeminacy, and carried with him the sciences of Greece. The Romans, in their career of glory, wrested their independence from the provinces they subdued, but in return they imparted laws, opulence, and civilization. Mahomet directed the tide of conquest over countries unworthy of freedom, and so abased in ignorance and barbarism, that even his religion and heroic mandates ennobled and enlightened them. The ravages of war in all those instances, were compensated by the splendour and security of the augmented monarchy. It was the ultimate design of the conqueror to establish his government in peace, and to disguise his military prowess in the beneficence of civil institutions.

The history of the world affords no instance of a power similar in principle, extent, and object, to that concentrated in the person of Napoleon. In his pursuit of imperial and universal supremacy, he regards neither the happiness of nations, the bonds of society, nor the terrors of futurity;

"Quem nec fama Deûm, nec fulmina, nec minitanti
"Murmure compressit cœlum."

With no title but that of the sword which he wields, he reigns over an immense population, diverted from all the pursuits of peaceful life, and taught by the spirit of all their institutions, that war is to be their habitual energy, and conquest their continual glory. To military service they sacrifice domestic feeling, personal gratification, and natural affection, and regard the honours of the camp, as the only means of particular advancement. The utmost terrors of an unrelenting conscription, the apprehension of dishonour, inseparably fixed by the law to the tranquil pursuits of industry and commerce, and extended from the reluctant individual to all his family, friends, and neighbours, with the hope of fame and brilliant reward, to be acquired in the tented field, impel the youthful mind to despise the peasant's lowly life, and make the empire of France a vast martial confederacy.

A patriotic pride characteristic of our country, with an attachment to civil authority and an enthusiastic love of liberty, derived from long experience of their benefits, inspires hatred rather than terror of the despot, who opposes his prodigious force to our independence, government, and civil freedom. A Briton will not disown that prejudice which renders him averse to the enemies of his sovereign; he will not sympathize with the arrogance and presumption of that warrior, whose glory is to be completed by our subjugation, and whose warfare, not carried on in generous rivalship, proceeds from malignant jealousy and ferocious pride. That philosophy which regards the love of our country as a vulgar and illiberal limitation of universal philanthropy, and would lower our national indignation at the pretensions, as well as the crimes of our aspiring foe, we shall consider as a fraudulent principle, which may weaken resistance and prop that ambition which it is our duty and interest to repress.

It is attributed to Louis the Fourteenth, that his wars were undertaken upon a project of universal domination, which he would inevitably have executed but for the energetic opposition of the grand alliance led by this country under King William, for the general safety of Europe. The success of that scheme would have been disgraceful and disastrous to the commonwealth of nations. Under all imaginable circumstances subjection to a foreign conqueror is degrading and oppressive. The noble sentiments of the heart are extinguished by the remembrance of defeat, and the pressure of inglorious bondage. The character of mankind vilified and debased in such humiliation, never soars to loyalty, honour, patriotism, or the admiration or practice of heroic virtue. Slavish submission, treachery, selfishness, cruelty, and meanness, are the qualities of those who tremble at a tyrant's frown, and flatter his vanity and pride.

Had Louis been able to accomplish his plan of universal monarchy, Europe, in the privation of its natural sovereigns, privileges and independence, would have sustained an irreparable calamity, but would not have incurred the lowest indignity of bondage. It would have passed under the rule of a prince, who acknowledged the obligations of law, and the restraints of piety. Afterwards his greatness was to be established, and his glory to result from the happiness and prosperity of all his people. Very different is the evil which the modern usurper would inflict on other states, and threatens to inflict on us. His triumph not only deprives the conquered nations of their laws, liberties, and independence, but fastens on them an unrelaxing tyranny which no laws can bind, which holds in no consideration the property and the lives of its subjects, and always acts by absolute merciless military despotism. All other monarchs have considered their glory augmented, and their strength consolidated by promoting the morals, prosperity, and happiness of the states they govern. Napoleon despises such antiquated policy. The temper which he cultivates is wholly and peculiarly that of savage warfare. The endearing, blandishments of peace he does not permit to assuage the hardihood of the soldier's stern contempt of danger. He only desires to be the leader of an unnumbered host, which bears his triumphant eagles through every region, and spreads the terror of his name among every people. Commerce, and the refinements of polished life he discourages, because they might arrest the ruffian hand of the undaunted warrior, and beget the gentler affections of our nature; but he permits and patronizes a gross licentiousness of manners, and an abandonment of morals, because they are consistent with that ferocious temper which favours his ruthless ambition, limited by no boundaries, and qualified by no beneficence.

The older governments of Europe, civil by institution, and in war tempered by justice and humanity, had encouraged those arts which refine the manners, and had established a moral community of interests, to reconcile, without destroying the national distinctions which appeared to separate mankind. Though ambition had sometimes disturbed the general harmony, and awakened the fears of an upright observer, as in the usurpations of Prussia and Russia, and the dismemberment of Poland, yet the proudest and most powerful of all the European sovereigns had abstained from making war the habitual temperament of mankind, and from incorporating with the rescripts of diplomacy, the language of defiance and hostile denunciation. Hostilities were considered and deprecated as the last unhappy result of opposing claims which negotiation could not balance, as the disease of the body politic, pernicious and destructive in its course. At every termination of hostilities, the contending sovereigns resumed a conciliatory and confidential intercourse, and the soldier was remitted to the ploughshare and the loom. An awful change has been effected by Napoleon. Europe will no more revert to that happy state and disposition, when society was secure in the faith of political engagements; when sovereigns with armies for a guard of honour, rather than for hostile preparation, were anxious to rule in love, and maintain their people in domestic peace and the pursuits of useful industry.

The conventions and promises of Napoleon, hardly pacific in denomination, do not quell the hostile mind, or allay the terror of his arms. In all circumstances he maintains alike his prodigious military establishment, composed of the whole population of France, always ready for aggression, and prepared in an instant to enforce his most arrogant demands. The main spring of his diplomacy is an army which vaunts itself to be irresistible and clamours for employment. The dreadful example imposes upon all other countries the necessity of equal preparation. That confidential intercourse from which the display of superiority, and the insolence of power were excluded, which diffused universally a spirit of concord and alliance, and extended the affections of philanthropy and brotherhood from one end of Europe to the other can never be restored. The new diplomacy, which substitutes violence for right, terror for humanity, and arrogant ferociousness for the dignified courage of our chivalrous institutions, is the work of the illustrious Napoleon.

Napoleon was welcomed to his imperial elevation by the aristocracy of talents. Under his despotism they expected to acquire, a second time, their predominance in the state. They anticipated that their aid would be solicited to maintain an usurpation which the ancient loyalist must scorn, the pure republican detest, the anarchist desire to overthrow, and the man of noble origin, or honorable mind, be ashamed to acknowledge. The emperor could only depend upon the support of his legions, and upon that of the opinion created in his favor by the men of letters and philosophers. He had no ancient nobility to claim his honors, no independent magistracy to participate in his power, no privilege to be opposed to his will. He was known to be vainly as desirous of eminence in literature and the sciences, as of martial glory and imperial power. He had declared himself a patron of learning and the arts. Secure of his favor, the literary republic lost no time in tendering to him their homage and adulation. They have attributed to him the valour of Alexander, the judgment of Cæsar, the philosophy of Antoninus, and whatever qualities of heroism, prudence, wisdom, and philanthropy ever augmented the splendor of a crown. The fancy of the painter and the poet, the art of the theatre, and the labor of the press, are all exerted to eulogize the power of the great monarch, to commend his taste, to magnify his glory, and to extol him for the admiration of a prostrate world.

The men of letters who had flourished, during the early uproar of the national assembly, and had opened the revolution with their speculations, the philosophers who had matured the important scheme at the hall of the jacobins, and in the national convention, all those who had borne the part of counsel in any period of the revolution; as many of them as had escaped the assassin's knife, and the sliver of the guillotine; planned, or eulogized the Consular and the Imperial Government, and have enjoyed its favor. Talleyrand, St. Jean D'Angely, Fouché, Mounier, Lameth, Rœderer, Sieyes, Barrere, David, Regnalt, and many others, were promoted to honor and employment. They were now willing to abstain from discussion of the rights of man, and the principles of natural equality; and they found, in the patronage of the First Consul and of the Emperor, other, and less perilous means of personal advancement. They no longer declaimed against the tyranny of all personal rule, and the barbarous oppression of privilege and distinction. They disputed no more of the propriety of the people, at pleasure, degrading their rulers, and passing judgment of death upon them by a process of national supremacy. Napoleon was able to suspend the knotty controversy of the contending parties. All claim to the nominal honor of combat they renounced in his favor; the idol of the golden calf of sovereignty, for which they had fought and bled, they yielded to him, but each was to receive from his bountiful hand the recompence of service:

"Non nostrum inter vos tantas componere lites;
"Et vitulâ tu dignus et hic:"

Each party was content with his decision and

liberal promise, and chaunted to the melody of imperial civism,

"Eris mihi Magnus Apollo."

Let it not be thought that all the professors of science, and the admirers of polite and useful literature, who flourish, and have flourished in this enlightened age, are united in counsel, or would participate in reward with that republic of letters which have attempted and attempts to disorganize society. This country has hitherto been peculiarly indebted to its poetry, its romance, and its philosophy. The moroseness and hypocrisy, which were once ingrafted into our character by the calamitous effects of the great rebellion, was pared away by the keen humour of Butler's immortal poem. That enthusiastic spirit of constitutional liberty, which ensured our protestant succession, was fanned to its utmost energy, when it seemed to languish, by the patriotic sentiments of the tragedy of Cato. A deep foundation of sound morality, combined with the elegancies of ornamental literature, was completed by the Spectator, the Guardian, and the Rambler. The coarseness and vulgarity of our old English squire was effectually cured by being faithfully exposed in the history of Tom Jones; and the model of a perfect gentleman, just without severity, polite without ostentation, and liberal without profusion; a character almost peculiar to the English nation, and to modern times, was successfully presented to imitation in the persons of Alworthy and Sir Charles Grandison. That general refinement of our principles and manners, in which the untainted modesty of the female sex is made essential to their loveliness and influence, was effected by the interesting tales of Pamela and Clarissa; while the licentiousness and impurity of the female character to which the savageness of the revolution may be in part attributed was, undoubtedly, much promoted on the continent, by the grossness, the intrigue, and the flimsy morality of the Maid of Orleans, the Emilius, and the new Eloisa.

But though our literature is still employed in accumulating treasures of useful knowledge and important truth, though in theology, ethics, history, science, and discoveries, the learned men who yet flourish among us have rendered their age illustrious, nevertheless it is impossible not to apprehend some pernicious effect from the wide diffusion of productions equally detrimental to sound religion, morality, and loyalty. Those whose understanding is matured, and whose taste is refined by liberal education, are gratified and instructed by new and important works, in every branch of human knowledge; but of the multitude, who read only the lighter productions of the day, how many derive all their morals from licentious romance, all their science from reviews and magazines, all their notions of government from the Political Register and disaffected pamphlets, and all their religion from the innumerable tracts of Calvinistic or Arminian doctrine, which are profusely distributed among the lower and unlettered classes. The tendency of all those publications is, of course, various and distinct; but their influence, whatever it may be, (and that it is inconsiderable no calm observer will assert) must be highly prejudicial to the manners, subordination, and rational piety of such as with better instruction may become the strength and ornament of society

In the universities of this kingdom, we still enjoy the example, and are benefited by the precepts of true philosophers, who, having explored the most secret recesses of nature, and weighed the heavens in a balance, have taught that the world was made in wisdom, and that unbounded goodness and design are apparent in the meanest offices of creation. They teach that our duties rest upon the basis of divine institution, that the christian revelation is able, and that it was ordained, to sustain the morals and the hopes of mankind, and that it is the only true and solid foundation of our social, moral, and religious obligations. We look to the parental government of this mighty country, with confidence, that its power will prevail against the gigantic efforts of its adversary. At the same time we confide in our venerable universities, and in all our other seminaries instituted for the promotion of piety and useful learning, with hope, that, under their fostering care, and liberal instruction, our youth may long be worthy of their illustrious ancestry; and that England, in distant times, may afford to the world a glorious example of power, exercised with justice, of science subservient to religion, of philosophy contributive to virtue, and of reason submissive to that revelation which surpasseth human understanding.

There are no means of creating or controuling the force of public opinion, equally efficacious with those afforded in the education of youth. The infant mind, unresisting and unsuspecting, may be tutored to virtuous sentiment and manly capability, or be perverted to base desire and slothful ignorance. We are taught the infinite importance of captivating the heart, while it is yet untainted by passion, and uninfluenced by error, in the example of one who, being wiser than the sons of men, commanded " that little children should be brought unto " him, and forbade them not." Though laws may be severe to detected criminals, and civil institutions be liberal in reward to ascertained merit, yet the influence of correct precept, infused into the youthful breast, is far more operative than the terror of punishment, or the more generous stimulant of hope.

The men of talent in France were equally aware of that powerful means of executing their peculiar project. While they introduced their savage doctrines into treatises of abstruse science, taste, and literature, they extended their influence, and secured their triumph, by empoisoning the sources of opinion in the establishments of education. It was the boast of Condorcet, " that " they made philosophy descend from the thrones " into the very universities." * Not satisfied with that success, they instituted their village schools, and, in the appointment of schoolmasters, paid from the royal treasury, they secured the corruption of the children of the peasantry. They thought it no degradation to lower their flight of philosophy, that they might have disciples in the humble dwellings of the husbandman and the artisan, and composed petty performances suited to the unlettered classes for cheap and gratuitous distribution, to corrupt the heart and the understanding of infants, to subvert the national religion, and to vilify the laws.

England is indebted, in no mean degree, for that liberality and consistency of sentiment, which

* Preface to his edition of Paschal's Thoughts, 1. Bar. Mcm. 3.

may perpetuate her freedom and her establishments, civil and religious, to a system of education, which was maintained among us by men eminent for learning, piety, and virtue, who flourished at the time of our reformation. Those illustrious fathers, who in persecution displayed the virtues of martyrdom, and at a happier period perfected an establishment which is dignified without impurity, and pious without fanaticism; and those who incorporated that establishment with the state, in union, and not merely by alliance; were indebted for their deep erudition, their rational religion, and their heroic patriotism, to that system of education, which yet flourishes among us: in which, learning is made the strong foundation of truth and knowledge, and in which, morality and piety, like inseparable sisters, concur in training the character to the utmost excellence which our frailty will permit us to attain.

The learned languages, which in the Political Register, are represented as worse than useless, in a system of general education, are a part of that foundation; not only because the acquiring of them is an exercise, which fortifies the understanding, and because they have a powerful influence to form the taste and ameliorate the temper of the heart, but because they contain the most splendid treasures of sound philosophy, the brightest examples of exalted virtue, the most liberal lessons of philanthropy and moral science, and the most decisive instances of the vigour of the human intellect: and, withal, they are an evidence of the necessity of wisdom superior to that of unenlightened nature, and strengthen our capacity to learn and comprehend the depth of that wisdom which cometh only from above.

If the love of classical literature, and that refinement of taste, which results from polite learning, be not a part of our virtue, yet they ennoble our habits, and embellish our manners. That heart is of mean conception, and vulgar feeling, which is not roused by the majesty of Homer, or the more temperate dignity of Virgil; which does not vibrate with loyalty, patriotism, and the sense of honor, in the contentions of the Iliad; which cannot sympathize with the sufferings of Ulysses, exemplary of patience, fortitude, contempt of voluptuousness, and degrading folly, and unyielding love of justice; or which does not mark with enthusiastic admiration the prudence, temperance, filial duty, and religious resignation of the pious Æneas. In the critical disquisitions of Aristotle and Longinus, the philosophy of Plato, the invigorating effusions of Demosthenes, the more polished eloquence of Cicero, and in all those productions of science and taste which illustrated the schools of Athens, and the Roman commonwealth, are deposited the principles of that knowledge, which enlarges and adorns the human understanding, gives new dignity to worldly honor, breaks the force of calamity, moderates the malignant passions, and kindles the virtuous affections. We must despise that ignorance or sloth which does not acknowledge the value of such resources, or omits to acquire them in their native mines, pure and unmixed in the servile process of translation; treacherous is that precept which would substitute for them the flimsy, unsubstantial fictions of modern philosophy, or the licentious poetry of the modern school. Ill-exchanged for that literature would be the language of the French academy, even as it was refined by the reforming philosophers, and its politics and morals as they are attempt[...] legislators [...]

The system of education, established in our public seminaries, is reprobated, not only by those who are incapable of estimating its value, or of imbibing its loyal and honorable sentiments; but, also, by a sect which is rapidly increasing among us; which begins to raise its clamour with formidable force, and seems to be actuated by principles similar to those of the Puritans and German anabaptists: a sect which originated in the vanity of presumptuous dogmatists, and has been, at all times, insolent in subjection, and intolerant in power.

In our schools we do not permit the speculations of casuistry to inflame the infant mind, at a time, when it is better disciplined in the pursuits of useful and ornamental knowledge and solid principle. We do not neglect the elements of religious doctrine, indispensable to complete the mental and moral character as they are provided in the church catechism with the illustrations of Secker, and with the aid of those manuals of rational and sound christianity, which our divines have prepared and adapted to the capacity of the infant understanding. We have also in use the Treatise of the learned Grotius *de veritate Religionis Christianæ.* Instead of the abstruser controversy, we put in the hands of our youth the volume of holy scripture; and in the simple precepts of christian morality, we think that we afford a system of divinity, practical rather than profound, far better suited to the untainted innocence of childhood, than that disputatious learning which seems less conducive to gentleness, diffidence, and love. We teach them that goodness is better than profession; that religion is not a matter of intellect, but a dispos   t   e art   t at benevolence is its basis and perfection; and that, though the mysteries of faith, and the hope of glory, are the evidences and the effect of pure and perfect piety, yet that charity which embraces whatever can pass by the name of virtue, is greater than these, and is the root and the flourishing branch of all true religion.

Happy will it be if a system of education, which has flourished under the safeguard of our social liberty, and the protection of our liberal church, may long continue to produce the luminaries of science, the defenders of religion, and the preceptors and patterns of morality. But while on the one hand it is undermined by the enemies of the constitution, and abused by the querulous advocates of infidelity, it is violated by a great confederacy who affect peculiar sanctity, make an ostentatious display of devout attitude and prostration, and arrogate to themselves "evangelical" distinction, even while they assail the solid foundations of practical beneficence. The power and the influence of that sect is widely extended by the means of education. Its schools, like those of the French philosophers, are raised in contemptuous opposition to the ministers of the national religion; their instruction is gratuitous, and is diffused by means of pamphlets and cheap publications, industriously circulated among the lower classes.

The tendency of their instruction is to create a sour, malignant, self-sufficiency; their little pupils are taught that the knowledge which we cultivate and value is the vanity of human wisdom, that the righteousness which we inculcate is as filthy rags, that our morality is impure and worthless, that the doctrine of which we treat in humility, and submission, as brought to be understood, and which our divines consider as too exalted for perfect understanding, is to be boldly preferred to our preceptive moral lessons, that it is better than piety, and will supply the want of active merit. Influenced by such tuition, the lower classes are made to think meanly of their superiors in fortune, function, and dignity, to despise the coercion of the laws, and to pant for that political change which is to elevate their sanctity, at least, to equality with merit recognized by law, and with profession ascertained by beneficence.

In the late proceedings of the Spanish nation, we shall, in vain, seek for any resemblance to the events and principles which have here been slightly sketched, as an historical summary of the Revolution in France. In Spain we have witnessed the energy of noble minds, displayed in patriotic language, to animate and to sustain the vigour of a great people struggling for independence in a cause of loyalty and national honour; but we have not heard of the pedantic effusions of false philosophy, conducive only to traitorous insurrection: there has been no disposition shewn, by means of violence, " to reduce
" the overgrown influence of the crown, to
" curb the pretensions of the privileged orders,
" to raise up the power of real talents and worth,
" to exalt the mass of the country, and to
" give them under the guidance of that aris-
" tocracy, to direct the councils of the country
" according to the spirit as well as the form"
of a revolutionary government. The exultation of the reviewers therefore is at least premature; if, unhappily, it were justified by events, such exultation would belong only to those who might share the honors of that aristocracy. But

in truth it would be of short duration. A revolution in Spain, or in England, brought about by such means, would infallibly proceed in like manner as did its prototype in France. The spirit of democracy, thus called again into active life, would rapidly degenerate into pure jacobinism. Then would commence another long and furious struggle between honor and infamy, opulence and pillage, power and rebellion, wisdom and vanity, public principle and the abomination of licence and misrule. That struggle would endure through a long period of terror and calamity, and must inevitably terminate in the establishment of a pure military despotism, under which the men of letters might have their little portion of disgraceful dependent patronage, but all other men of civil rank and function must groan in hopeless bondage and affliction. ' Such a revolution has not been attempted in Spain, and to that circumstance, the author of the Political Register attributes the triumph of the usurper, and the discomfiture of the patriotic forces. The usurper's triumph may be of short duration; and the patriotic forces may by many instances of success, similar to their early victories and to that recent glory achieved at Vigo, shew that though driven from the field, they may rally and must at last prevail. Such is the hope and confidence' of this county, in firm alliance with Ferdinand VII. It remains now to inquire whether the English constitution in its principles, or abuses, is become so oppressive, that we stand in need of " the reform, the radical " change, and revolution," recommended by the Edinburgh Reviewers, in order "to raise up among " us, the power of real talents and worth."

END OF PART II.

THE RIGHTS OF THE SOVEREIGNTY.

PART THE THIRD.

IN the year 1235, when the bishops proposed to the Lords of Parliament, that the canon law should be accepted in England, in lieu of the antient laws and constitution, we are told in the language of the antient statute, "omnes comites "et barones unâ voce responderunt quod nolunt "leges Angliæ mutari quæ usitatæ sunt et appro- "batæ." *

At that early period the English nation rejected all change upon speculative principle. The accustomed and approved law which they had received from their fore-fathers by a title of inheritance, and by long experience had found to be beneficial, they would not yield to the counsel of the learned prelates, who attempted to introduce into this country the laws then recently adopted in foreign nations, and by the means of that reformation, were supposed to aim at personal rule, and to claim the pre-eminence of an aristocracy of talents.

That proposed innovation was not in favour of crude and speculative principle; unsanctioned by

* Statute of Merton, 20 Hen. III. The direct proposal of the Bishops was to legitimatize children born before marriage, their object to introduce the authority of the canon laws.

experience and unpromising of beneficial result. It was in deference to a system of laws compiled upon the basis of that admirable code, which the Roman jurists had skilfully adapted to all the necessities of their vast and flourishing empire; and had constructed for the imitation and applause of all civilized communities. That code had been already made the basis of jurisprudence by every other European monarchy; its beneficial effects upon the progress of learning, the refinement of manners, the establishment of moral equality in the administration of justice, and the correcting the barbarous institutions of that savage race which had founded the western nations, is not to be denied. Its unimpaired authority in many enlightened states, and the respect with which its maxims are regarded, wherever reason and equity are admitted to co-operate in the ministration of civil justice, are an evidence of its intrinsic excellence. In this country we are impelled by natural feeling, and are bound by the unshaken judgment of many ages, to extol the unrivalled superiority of our own laws, in comparison with whatever form or system of social polity the wisdom of sages has imagined or the world has witnessed. But we should be wanting in gratitude to the clergy of that dark period if we did not commend and venerate their zeal and unwearied diligence, their learning and philanthropy, their love of order and moral discipline, by which they gradually subverted, in the states of the continent, the customs and institutions of feudal barbarism and effectuated the revival of that general jurisprudence, which after the darkness of ignorance and oppression, came as the early dawn of literature and science, and led in a succeeding age to the meridian splendour of government, social freedom, and universal civilization.

In a far happier condition was the English nation. Its laws and customs, however compounded, or from whatever source derived, were of high antiquity: They were not committed to a perishable record, but were deeply engraven in the hearts of a virtuous and heroic people. They had subsisted immemorially; they had weathered the rude shock of the Norman conquest, and were endeared to every order, because they were universally known, and were excellently adapted to their wants, their affections, their innate prejudices, and their acquired habits. They had long flourished under the supremacy of a potent monarch, whose greatness was essential to the vigour of public justice, and to the energy of a martial race, but was restrained by numberless controuling checks from violating the privileges of the superior ranks, or entrenching on the franchises of the lower. They were the natural growth of that antient spirit of liberty which had animated the whole body of the state; and while it had confirmed their due weight and consideration to wealth, and to noble origin, had made the poor man's cottage his castle of defence, unassailable by violence and unimpregnable by lawless power. As the work and labour of a remote ancestry, who were independent, bold, and provident, the people of that day regarded them with pious veneration; they valued them as a rich inheritance, to be loved with a generous pride when enjoyed in tranquil times, and to be valiantly defended, if occasion required, with life itself. They considered it as not less than a natural obligation, and an important branch of their parental duty, to transmit inviolate, to their children, the same laws and customs, which might for ever pass as the birthright of the country; to be prized for its incomparable excellence, and to be revered for its distant origin.

Not many years before that period, the great charter of England had been obtained by the same patriotic nobles, actuated by the same attachment to the antient laws and institutions. By that memorable statute created as a perpetual barrier against the arbitrary power of a prince, among various other franchises connected with the feudal forms of the constitution at that time prevailing, the freedom which we now enjoy was fundamentally enacted. To all the municipalities of the realm, were conceded their antient liberties and customs. (cap. ix.) And by the most compendious legislative provision upon record, the liberty of the person, the security of property, the supremacy of the law, the trial by jury, with the full, free, and prompt administration of justice and of right, which seem to be the cardinal points of the glorious constitution under which we have the happiness to live, were amply secured. (Cap. xxix.) " Nullus liber
" homo capiatur vel imprisonetur aut disseisiatur
" de libero tenemento suo vel libertatibus vel
" liberis consuetudinibus suis, aut utlagetur aut
" exulet aut aliquo modo destruatur, nec super eum
" ibimus nec super eum mittemus, nisi per legale
" judicium parium suorum, vel per legem terræ.
" Nulli vendemus nulli negabimus aut differemus
" rectum vel justitiam."

It was in favour of such laws, the early boast of our country, that the admirable union of government and freedom was confirmed, at a time when other nations were coerced by power, and accepted wholesome restraint as the grace of magistracy. It was for such a system that our ancestors proclaimed, " quod nolunt leges Angliæ mutare."

During the lapse of six hundred years, the wisdom displayed in the Parliament of Merton, has been unquestioned and revered. In all the contests of a doubtful succession, of resisance to oppression, of religious innovation, and every other instance of political contention, which our eventful history commemorates, that wisdom seems to have been the active principle of every national proceeding. It was not permitted by our ancestors to be deduced by inference, nor to appear only in the annals of their age, as a fact of historical importance. When they established their own system of law, in preference to that which next to their own, every nation has regarded as the wisest and the best, they did not suffe rtheir resolution to pass, like all other matters of negation, without legislative memorial; they caused it to be recorded among the statutes of the realm, that they would *not* change the accustomed and approved laws, and gave an example of attachment to the constitution, which has been observed in all subsequent transactions; hitherto, whatever violations of liberty might have followed the ambitious projects of an usurpation, or the violent outrage of a rebellion, or the fatal zeal of a religious persecution; in their temporary triumph; in all those circumstances, the national sentiment has remained unaltered. That reverence to our noble progenitors, which naturally makes the mind of heroic and loyal temper like their's, a feeling rather than a judgment, with which we were inspired when our infant hearts were first impressed to admire and to imitate great and virtuous example, has hitherto been the characteristic quality of our nation. It is altogether novel among us to assert a different principle in our domestic politics, to impair and to calumniate that inborn reverence, and to raise the recent clamour for radical reform, for change, and for revolution.

If that choice of our illustrious ancestors was unwise and improvident; if they ought to have clipped the wings of royal prerogative which are said to overshadow the liberties of the people, and to have taught their king, that so far from enjoying an independent supremacy, conferred by the constitution, to protect and to consolidate the rights of the nation, he was no more than a servant of the state with a delegated and responsible trust; if they ought to have abandoned their own privilege and distinction, which are incompatible with an equality of rights, and to have submitted to the rule and direction of that natural democracy in which we are now told an unalienable sovereignty is vested; in that case let us abandon the instruction of history; let us deprecate that example which our fathers, the slaves of prejudice, commanded us to revere; and let us reprobate as injustice and usurpation, that very proceeding, which we have been taught to applaud as a glorious effort of honour and virtue, because it gave stability to the liberties of the subject, by uniting them in right and title to the lawful authority of the prince.

That liberty which is the foundation and the golden summit of our British constitution, as it was ordained by the oldest statute of the realm, our lawgivers certainly did not derive from " the bulk and " the mass of the people, of the multitude, and of " the mob itself." During the long period in which the course of legal franchise has fertilized, strengthened, and adorned, the native soil of Englishmen; it has proceeded in a pure and tranquil current; not turbid and tempestuous, like that which originates in the violent and outrageous gulph of wild democracy; but calm, salutary, and auspicious, like that which derives its source from wisdom, order, and the law. If the choice of the multitude, and of the mob, be the only legitimate spring of social liberty, then our uninstructed ancestors were mistaken in their constitutional provisions; and we their descendants being blessed with a purer doctrine, and initiated into a sounder philosophy, should no longer perpetuate their errors, nor exult in the beneficence of their politic regulations.

Then we may cease to extol the patriotism of an Alfred, the valour of an Edward and a Henry, the prudence of an Elizabeth, and the sageness and the heroism of King William. The virtues which have so often illustrated the royal line, and illumine our English annals, can no more be of practical advantage. Then we shall no more commend the firmness, the vigour, the loyalty, and the love of liberty, which formed the character of our antient nobles. Those who shall acquire greatness in the new regimen by less honorable qualities, (for in every form of society, some men will acquire greatness) cannot be stimulated by their example, nor by their hope of dignity, to assert like them the lawful rights of every order, in contempt of the unlawful pretensions of a tyrannizing power; nor like them to lead the gallant armies of the country in defiance of difficulty and danger, to wrest by manly enterprize, from a presumptuous enemy, the palm of victory and glory. Then we may no longer search for lessons of jurisprudence in the proceedings of our venerable judges, who maintained the pre-eminence of the law over all privilege and prerogative, and rendered our English courts the sanctuaries of truth and justice. Then the elaborate writings, which were compiled to illustrate and perpetuate the excellent provisions of our unwritten law, and the great volume of our statutes, with Magna Charta, and the bill of Rights, and the act of Habeas Corpus, and the act of Settlement, and all the other ordinances which parliaments have in wisdom provided to establish our liberties on a solid foundation, may be abrogated and annulled. Then we shall no more boast of an inheritance derived from an ancestry, who matured the constitution by deliberative counsel, who gloriously contended for it in battle, and thought it the noblest reward of their success, when they left it perfect for our enjoyment. Their hallowed tombs, rudely emblazoned by trophies of generous heroism, achieved in the service of their sovereign, we shall no longer approach with reverential awe; we shall not pant for opportunity to emulate their virtues; and we shall despise as romantic fiction, the engraven records of their fame.

In the flood of light, which the aristocracy of talents will open, the beneficence of kings, the virtues of nobles, the wisdom of judges, the providence of parliaments, the force of great example, and all the lessons of experience, will become as the remnant of an obsolete superstition, the ridicule of reformers, and the contempt of triumphant innovators. The modern philosophy will discover that patriotism was unknown in England, till it shall then appear in the form of insurrection, under the guidance of the new aristocracy. The doctrine of the rights of the people, to exalt the mass of the community under that guidance, shall beggar the wisdom of all our progenitors, and shall show that they, with the means of acquiring perfect freedom, were content to temperate a power which was radically oppressive, and which, however moderated, can only exist as a distemper, as a nuisance, and a violation of natural right.

Such may be the opinions of those who invite

our people to disaffection and conspiracy. They may not fear a comparison of their own intelligence and pretensions, with all the wisdom, the prudence and the loyalty, which have benefited this illustrious nation from Alfred's day to the present, to govern and influence its counsels. They may fondly imagine that the smartness of repartee, the quaintness of humour, the facetiousness of satire, the keenness of reproach; or to give higher commendation, where it may be claimed, that the grave discussions of scientific and philosophical researches, compiled for the editor of the Edinburgh Review, and the sturdy declamation of the Political Register, will, in the public judgment, hold an advantageous competition with the qualities of all the statesmen, patriots, warriors, and advocates of legal order, who reared and embellished the British constitution as it is now by law established. Anxious at whatever risque, to enter upon the important duties of making and administering laws, they may believe themselves well qualified to act in all the various relations of our foreign and domestic policy; disdaining the labours of their less bold precursors in the art of government, they may be willing to level at one blow; a fabric venerable for its duration of at least a thousand years, and will "extra-" "vagantly rejoice" at an opportunity to proclaim their new constitution, which they have pilfered, with their declaration of rights, from the philosophers of the Paris committees, and the legislators of the revolutionary tribunal.

But such are not yet the opinions of the British public. They will not so hastily condemn as unwise and improvident, the choice of our ancestors, hitherto approved and confirmed by the choice of all their posterity. Illuminated as we are by the new notions of philosophy and national policy, not one of which can be deduced from the practice or the principles of our forefathers, we shall pause before we enter upon that work of destruction, by which alone our modern theory can be put to experiment. Even though that natural piety, which sanctifies the precepts and the example of the illustrious dead, may no longer hold its rank among the civic duties, yet, in prudence if not in virtue, we shall estimate the value of the inheritance we possess, and endeavour to calculate the advantages of the rights we are invited to assume. Though, on the one side, there is nothing but promise and possibility, and perhaps little chance of ultimate benefit, and no security at all, yet we shall not conclude the bargain till we have deliberated upon the price to be paid for the distant and contingent amelioration.

In that deliberation it will first occur to us, that a foundation for the inquiry ought to be laid in grievance, unlawful, hopeless, and oppressive. The constitution established, was designed for the redress of all ordinary grievance; and has even by that memorable event of 1688, provided a remedy for the most extreme case of oppression and usurpation, which is recorded in our annals. If the existence of the monarchy be necessarily oppressive, if the legislative faculty of the three estates be an intolerable grievance, if the establishment of the church, and the administration of justice, by the king's appointed delegates, be naturally an abuse of public rights, then let our modern reformers openly avow, that it is their object to abrogate the monarchy, to destroy the functions of parliament, to overthrow the church, to annul the authority of magistrates, and to establish a new constitution, suited to their own notion of propriety and right. For all other grievances the subsisting constitution has provided appropriate remedy, by means of those same institutions. But when the Edinburgh Reviewers propose " to exalt the mass of the community, " and to give them under the guidance of the " aristocracy of talents, to direct the councils " of England," and qualify their proposal by adding, " that it is according to the spirit as well " as the form of our invaluable constitution," it is an insinuation, false, impudent, and treacherous. That constitution is invaluable, because it has provided its remedies, for every possible grievance, without recurring, in any case, to the mass of the community; because, in all ordinary cases, those remedies are found in the orderly exercise of the functions of parliament; because, in an extreme case, a remedy will be found in the right of resistance, to be then only exercised in the last necessity, by the constituted authorities of the realm, and never in any case vesting in the mass of the community.

Let those who would " extravagantly rejoice" in that assumption of right by the multitude and the mob, candidly avow, that instead of acting under the sanction of the British constitution, they assert a principle never imagined by our ancestors, and destructive of our laws. Let them know that " as far as in them lays, " they are a party to revolutionary measures."

It is better to meet the question fully, and to consider whether or not the British constitution as transmitted to us, be a nuisance and an oppression; and whether or not, on the ground of grievance, we stand in need of any sort of remedy to be afforded by the mass of the community.

In that inquiry we shall find that all the important purposes for which government can be constituted, or liberty be valued, are in this country abundantly enjoyed, and effectually secured. We have, in its highest possible degree, that right of personal security, which consists in the legal and uninterrupted enjoyment of life, limbs, body, health, and reputation. Our personal liberty is not less sacred in the consideration of our law; so that we have no functionary, howsoever potent, who can, with impunity, impose the least unlawful restraint upon the meanest subject of the realm, either by colour of justice, or in open violation of its rules. The right of property is so sacred, that no pretence of state necessity can justify the sovereign himself, for the smallest exaction, either to maintain the dignity of his power, or to support the authority of his government, without the sanction of the estates of the realm in parliament assembled. Our taxation heavy, as we think it, is admitted to be lighter than that of any other country in Europe; with a system of collection infinitely less vexatious and oppressive.* The freedom of the press, terrible to all tyranny, and incompatible with all abuse of power, is among us so sacred, that it is permitted to approach to licentiousness, and that every week, without legal interference, we are offended by an obtrusion of opinions and assertions the most seditious, scandalous, and false. Our religious toleration is complete. No man is questioned for any sentiments, religious or political, which are not

* See the last No. of the Edinburgh Review, 449. That fact simply stated, might be an appropriate motto to the list of the 125 members of Mr. Wardle's minority, which Mr. Cobbett " will have printed upon fine and stout paper, ca-" pable of being *framed*, so that it may be hung up, and " read a————efore the fire." See the Political Register, 1st April, 1809.

immediately destructive of the peace of society, and do not endanger the public safety. What other nation can boast of equal franchises? Will the new philosophy afford us more substantial liberty? For the perpetual defence and preservation of all these rights, we have the security of parliament, the ascertained limitations of the royal prerogative, the unsuspected purity of public justice, the privilege of petitioning the throne, and the two houses of the legislature, upon any imputed grievance, or any apparent necessity; and what was never elsewhere entrusted to the subject under any form of government whatever, but is here sanctioned and declared by a fundamental statute, * " that the subjects, " which are protestants, may have arms for their " defence, suitable to their condition, and as " allowed by law."

Our hereditary monarchy is endued with ample prerogative. The sovereign has not only the power of calling into action the legislative estates, but it is by his assent alone, that their decision acquires the force of law. From him is derived the whole of the judicial function, and in his person is vested entire the executive branch of government. The public expenditure is exclusively under his direction: he has the sole command of the public forces, military and maritime: to him belongs the management of all foreign relation, both in war and peace. In the exercise of these attributes, he owes responsibility to none. But, nevertheless, the constitution has provided, with sufficient care, that he shall be powerful, only for the public good; and that in the ministration of his high office he shall, not only by

---

* Declaration of Rights. 1 William and Mary, c. 2.

construction of law, but from absolute necessity, be incapable of doing wrong. His ministers and advisers are, without exception, responsible for his transgression, and are amenable for obeying his unlawful mandates. They are not less answerable for their counsel, if it be detrimental to the public interest; and can never plead the royal prerogative for measures illegal or impolitic. If the policy, which the monarch will pursue, be plainly adverse to the sentiments of the nation, or, if he persevere in retaining ministers, who do not enjoy the confidence of parliament, the Commons have the means of dictating, even in the exercise of his prerogative, by withholding the ordinary supplies. The potency of his sceptre is as weakness, and the splendor of his crown is of faded lustre, without the aid and approbation of his parliament. He has no force to maintain his vast prerogative, much less to invade the rights of his people, without that supply which he can only obtain from the beneficence of his parliament.

But it is said that the sovereign may accomplish, by influence, that which he dares not attempt by prerogative; and the Edinburgh Reviewers would " extravagantly rejoice in any con-
" ceivable event which should reduce the over-
" grown influence of the crown."

The history of the reign of the present sovereign, in which that influence is said to have arrived at prodigious excess, will confute the charge. Was the monarch able to overcome Mr. Wilkes, an obscure individual, though the whole power of the state was directed against him. " The rays of royal indignation, collected upon
" him, served only to illuminate, but could not
" consume." * Could the undivided power of go-

* Junius's Letter to the King

vernment, sanctioned by the votes of parliament, and upheld by popular opinion, avail against the persons charged with treason, in 1794. The accused persons had the benefit of the law, and rested upon the trial by jury. However guilty, upon that rock they defied the prosecution, and were placed where no influence has yet attempted to obtain conviction without conclusive evidence, to distort the truth, or to pervert the judgment.

Complaint is made of the influence of the crown in the deliberations of parliament. Five-and-twenty years ago, the House of Commons asserted, not without censure, that such influence existed;* that to a certain degree it does exist, it would be vain to deny; perhaps, it is irrational to lament. It may be a benefit, instead of an injury, to the commonwealth, and ought not to be condemned till it is found detrimental.

The members of a popular assembly, always capable, by means of its privileges, of usurping the powers of sovereignty, subject to the impulse of faction, and naturally controuled or led by the spirit of its most aspiring leaders, must be always liable to tumult and aggression. However constituted, whether composed of men who sit by hereditary right, or are delegated by popular election, having the means at pleasure, of grasping the emoluments, and of claiming the dignity of office, and of exercising the attributes of government, some part of that assembly must be subject to absolute restraints, or be guided by gentler means; otherwise they will, at some time or other, be actu-

* By the vote made on Mr. Dunning's motion " that the " influence of the crown had increased, was increasing, and " ought to be diminished."

ated by that ambition of which societies are not less susceptible than individuals. All the members of the House of Commons were, at one time, strictly independent. Its pretensions advanced in constant opposition to the monarch; and at last it aimed, with complete success, at the dissolution of the state, and at arrogating to itself all the authority and the revenues of government. The acknowledged prerogative of King Charles, was not less extensive than that at present appertaining to the crown. That unfortunate prince, with whatever reluctance, yielded to the republican ardour which grew out of the absolute independence of the Commons, and at last made every concession which was necessary to their constitutional freedom, or compatible with any limitation of royalty. But they would be satisfied with no concessions. Possessing the treasure of the nation, and allowing none of it to go in aid of the king's government; being desirous of permanent and independent power, they proceeded step by step, till they compelled their sovereign to become their rival, their enemy, their prisoner, and their victim; and till all privilege and franchise of the subject was their sport and plunder.

After the restoration, the members of the house were equally independent of the influence of the crown. The prince became jealous of their privileges. A contest ensued between prerogative, which aimed at tyranny, and the just rights of parliament. That contest terminated in the happy accession of King William, when the greatness of the sovereign, and the privileges of the legislature were made compatible, and were permanently united in a beneficial concord.

" If parliament lost any portion of its collective independence, or were subject to the mandate of the sovereign, the essential vigour of the constitution would be lost, and the forms of liberty would only serve to bring to painful recollection the inestimable blessing which we had lost. The Roman Senate, though in abased servility, survived the liberties of their country, but being subject to a stern master, they only served to reconcile the degraded country to the galling yoke of personal despotism. It was by the collision of parties, and the triumph of faction in that august assembly, that the public mind was prepared for the practical subversion of the Roman constitution. If, in the House of Commons, there was no one by influence or interest, bound to maintain its harmony with the other branches of the legislature, vehement opposition might soon arise out of relentless faction; liberty would be lost in the conflicts of party; and government must soon assume the character of an absolute monarchy, or of a less tolerable oligarchy.

It may be said, that a House of Commons, subject to such influence, is but an organ of royalty, a delusive phantom of public liberty, and an unnecessary incumbrance to the state. Such it would be, most truly, if its decisions were dictated by the crown, and its deliberations controuled by authority. But that influence to which some of its members are subject, is limited; and cannot be directed beyond the ordinary administration of affairs. It can never aim at any object injurious to the public welfare, or at any increase of the royal power; but is naturally and invariably confined to those objects which are strictly within the view and intention of the British constitution.

It is a maxim of that constitution, that the King shall have the appointment of the executive servants of the state. If the members of the House of Commons were all of them unconnected with any interest but that of their own house, would they not more frequently assume the right to which a minority is always devoted, and at which, once at least in the present reign, a majority directly aimed; that of controuling the King's nomination, and of imperiously fixing their own leading members in the several departments of office? Would the ministers appointed by the vote, and dependent upon the favor of that house be most solicitous of serving the king, their nominal master, or of obtaining popular applause, and the continued support of their constituent majority? In such a case the honor of the crown would be titular, and its power extinct; while the nation, instead of the security of a powerful and permanent administration, responsible to parliament, would be governed by ministers, constituted by the House of Commons, without any responsibility, and without any possibility of long retaining their appointment; and all parties would be perpetually distracted by the uproar and the disorders, inseparable from a state of faction, and political contention.

Those who lament that the members of the House of Commons are some of them subject to royal influence, should examine the human heart before they proceed to complaint and censure. Do they fondly believe that a numerous body, drawn promiscuously by any process of delegation, from any order of society, shall possess, individually, intelligence and virtue to be placed above delusion or indirect controul? In what age or country, under any imaginable mode of formation, has such an assembly been constituted? In the common affairs of life, for the management of municipal transactions, or of village-interests, wherever independent power is lodged in a numerous meeting, some leader invariably arises, whom it would be ridiculous to honour as possessing a purer heart, or a more able understanding, than those who submit to his direction. The nature of man is not changed by elevated rank, or by political function. That spirit of intrigue, faction, and ambition, which distracts the vestry of a parish, and the corporation of a borough, will actuate the heart of the legislator and the statesman. To complain that every individual member of parliament does not rest upon his own intelligence and knowledge, is to betray a gross ignorance of the faculties and temper which are common to all mankind. To raise an outcry, that some men are influenced by the authority of a government which has shewn itself just and patriotic, while praise is bestowed upon others who oppose that government by a slavish adherence to a leader of factious principles and unsuccessful ambition, plainly shews, that aversion to the established authority occasions the objection; and that such complaint would cease when that authority should yield to opposition.

The royal influence never yet maintained a minister who wanted other free support, nor ever protected his conduct from the strict and hostile inspection of a vigilant opponent; who being once able to affix stigma to his name, or to impute to him the least corruption or malversation, instantly became the leader of a triumphant majority. The influence of office, the support of an unsuspected coadjutor, the weight of personal friendship, and the merit of laborious duty, were all insufficient to rescue Lord Melville from accusation and public trial, when suspicion of corrupt transaction was raised against him. The recent investigation of criminal charges brought against a distinguished member of the royal house, is another conclusive proof, that, of whatever nature the influence of the crown may be, it can shelter no man, of whatever power or rank, from that parliamentary inquiry which a public accuser demands.

The free sanction of parliamentary confidence is necessary to the support of every minister; for without it no one has yet attempted to maintain himself in the service of the King. The abdication of Sir Robert Walpole, and the frequent changes which followed that abdication in the last reign; the versatility of counsel during the earlier part of the present reign; the resignation of Lord North; the failure of the famous coalition; and the secession of Mr. Addington's ministry, all shew that the influence of the crown is not paramount; and that it cannot controul the sense of parliament when plainly hostile to any administration. That sense is not always declared by a majority of votes, but is sometimes not less equivocally expressed; and when it is evidently evinced, the most resolute minister must yield his own judgment, and conform to measures prescribed by his opponents. In the vigour of his power, Mr. Pitt was guided by that sense, when he assented to the repeal of the shop-tax, his earliest and favorite project of finance; and, six years afterwards, when he submitted to the policy of his rival, and assented to the peace between Turkey and Russia, upon terms which he thought incompatible with the interests of this country. By the sense of parliament was dictated the dismemberment of the empire at the acknowledgement of the independence of America. The peace of Amiens, fruitful of those disasters against which we at present struggle, was made in obedience to the sense of parliament. The act of the last session for limiting the patronage of the crown, in the grant of reversionary appointments, was obtained by the House of Commons in direct opposition to the former sentiments of the sovereign, of his ministers, and of the upper house. The constituting of the various committees to inquire into the ministration of every public department, is a proof that, at this instant, whatever the influence of the crown may be, it cannot check that investigation of abuses, which is an important parliamentary function.

Let those who complain of that influence in parliament maintain their cause, by shewing actual grievance, occasioned by its exercise. If they can shew that from the operation of that cause, the Commons have neglected their important duties; that they have lent their aid for the persecution of innocence, or for the protection of convicted guilt ; that they have assented to measures of injustice or oppression, or omitted to dictate measures of justice and public utility; if they have permitted the laws to be violated, foreign war to be prosecuted for vain glory, or fatal ambition ; or domestic advantages to be sacrificed to personal interest, prejudice, or humour ; if they have abandoned, in a single instance, their own privileges, or one item of the public liberties, then that complaint may not be without foundation: but while that influence shall be usefully applied for constitutional purposes, and shall never be directed to oppression or national detriment, so long we may hope that the public ear will be deaf to such complaint. The argument may be well-suited to those shallow understandings, which are not satisfied with solid and permanent utility, without external form and splendour; it is still better adapted to those whose object it is, not to renovate, but to destroy the constitution; who would overlook its conveniencies and advantages, calumniate whatever differs from their peculiar theory, and represent as defective and pernicious, whatever is opposed to their scheme and policy. It will never be adopted by those who consider that the great end of all government is the public good, and will be satisfied with an institution which is found conducive to that important end.

When the passions of mankind shall be subdued by reason, and the understanding, unclouded by error, shall be called to deliberate and resolve unbiassed by vanity and interest; (a period, which the past measures of reformers have not seemed to accelerate;) then it may become a practical principle of the British constitution, that every individual member of the lower house shall be in personal independence, not only of the crown, but of the nation which he represents. The complaint of influence has been chiefly applied to that of the King and of his ministers; and all those who have composed the majority in favor of any system of administration, are despised as the slaves of power, or the corrupt tools of interest. But there is another influence by which the deliberations of parliament are swayed. There are pretended patriots who, impelled by more dangerous ambition, will sacrifice duty and judgment to acquire the support of popular applause. Will such men, when they gain the palm for which they contend, be still the advocates of public liberty? Or, will they not, as in former instances, when possessed of the power of the state by means of their popularity, cease to be panders to the vices of the people? Will not they, too, show that intrigue and corruption are complained of by reformers without sincerity? and, that when the favor of the multitude can no longer serve the purposes of the aspiring demagogue, he, too, will be an advocate of power, and call for confidence and submission?

Knowledge, foresight, prudence, and virtue, are necessary to qualify the independent legislator for his important duty. Where shall we find, in society, six hundred men known to be entitled by such qualities, to regulate the affairs of the British empire; and if they were found, by what means shall we obtain their delegation to parliament by any description of constituents. Such men will not flatter the ignorant and tumultuous multitude of electors; which, as it should be more numerous by an extension of the elective franchise, would become more ignorant and tumultuous. They will not stoop to the base contrivances of an election contest, nor court the grovelling passions of the vulgar, by traducing the state, and scandalizing rank and property. They will not make promises of public benefits, improper to be made, and impossible to be performed; nor will they represent the necessary restraints of law as violations of the constitution, and of the natural rights of man. Against them the more loquacious popular candidate has an incalculable advantage. His professions are liberal, because they are insincere, and his interest is powerful because he applies to the venal and corrupt.

It is altogether hopeless, that parliament should be wholly composed of men, whose exalted virtue and enlightened minds render them above controul and influence, and superior to error. The senate being tinctured with the frailty of human nature, never can be exempt from those motives which actuate the heart in every relation of life. Constituted as in this country, it is directly exposed to the influence of two opposing powers, that of the crown on the one side, and of the people on the other.

The influence of the crown, whatever it may be, like the prerogatives attached to the regal office, is administered by persons who are responsible for the use to which they apply it, and are personally interested in making only such application of it as may be consistent with the public service. By becoming the servants of Government, they are not deprived of their personal interest in the privileges of parliament, and the liberties of the subject. By those privileges they may chiefly hope, permanently, to possess their high situations; for, in the appointment of ministers, the confidence of the commons has been known to outweigh the predilection of the King. Deprived of that support, their master might become their tyrant, and their only remaining security would be the continued favor of a prince, who might not only drive them from office, but subject them to the disgrace of Wolsey, and the martyrdom of More. Ministers can never be indifferent to those franchises in which they have an interest in common with all their fellow subjects; and it is highly improbable, that parliament can ever be induced, by such influence, to concur in any violation of the constitution. The members have a more direct personal interest even than ministers, to preserve it unimpaired; and by conceding it to an ambitious sovereign, they would not only lose their share in the liberties of the country, but more immediately the pre-eminence of their legislative function, with all security of life, rank, and property. Nor would a scheme so fatal and foolish be undertaken by parliament itself, with any probability of success. That popular opposition, which in former instances, has prevailed over the united opinions of government and the legislature, would instantly become more vigorous, and would ultimately triumph in a contest, destructive of all those who had rashly and wickedly provoked it.

The influence of the people may, even now, be perceived in parliament. How many accusations of distinguished merit, aspersions of honorable character, proposals of insecure peace, and projects of dangerous innovation, have proceeded from that cause. If it were ever to prevail over the influence of constituted authority, it would be administered without discretion, justice, or understanding. Subject to deception, versatility, and humour; and called into energy by insidious demagogues, its dictates would be rash and perilous. The common restraints of government, which the multitude often deem oppressive, they would require to be moderated or abandoned. The policy of important and necessary warfare, not understood by them, they would, by the direction of servile adulators, like the Athenian orators, in the pay of a foreign enemy, reprobate and counteract. Their judgment, seldom impartial and enlightened, would commonly be directed by passion, caprice, and vengeance. The parliament subject to such influence must, like them, be unjust, capricious, and vindictive. No administration could be strong, permanent, or prudent; society must perpetually be convulsed by contending factions, and the constitution must soon yield to the hostility of aspiring democrats.

The editor of the Weekly Register, vehemently complains of the admission of the king's ministers and other servants of state, to sit in the House of Commons, and at a late election, where he was entitled to a vote, he demanded of the candidates a pledge that they would never accept of office under his majesty, if they should obtain the representation of the county of Hants.

The exclusion of the king's ministers would give to the electors the nomination of ten or twelve persons less immediately connected with the crown, than those who bear the high offices of state. Is it probable that any important public question, to be decided by a division, would depend essentially upon that nomination? The editor of the Weekly Register will hardly advance so ridiculous a position. If a constitutional jealousy of ministers will justify the excluding of those twelve persons from having voices in the legislature, it ought to proceed much further than to banish them from parliament, and not to stop till a government is established, the members of which may have, at least, as much confidence and respectability as the nominee of the Duke of Bedford, or any other borough-proprietor, or as the champion of popular rights, deputed by the electors of Westminster. A government, which is not only to be watched but to be suspected, and without proof of malversation, or the formality of a criminal charge, to be mistrusted, and to be shut out from the great council of the nation; and that not to produce any beneficial effect in the proceedings of parliament (for that cannot be pretended) but to impress upon the public mind, that it never should confide in those whom the sovereign has selected on account of their wisdom and their ascertained merits, to assist him in the exercise of his duties; such a government had better be at once superseded. Ministers that are not loved, honored, or respected; that are to attend the legislature in a capacity of servitude, without partaking of its privileges or functions; that when questioned, are to stand at its bar, rather as criminals than as having in their hands the exercise of the royal power, and are there to wait the scorn, reviling, and accusation of every vain pretender to political science, and of every candidate for popular esteem, bound to silent and indignant submission, till the house shall permit them to assert their innocence, or to defend their ministration; such a body of men must be inadequate to the purposes of their institution. Their tempers being soured by reproach to which they must not reply, and full of resentment for insults offered through them to the crown itself, they can never love that parliament; but if they have the courage and understanding, which in their situations they ought to have, they may think that they afford to their master faithful service, by advising him to render his authority independent of that harsh and unmannerly controul.

Ministers admitted to the legislature, are now anxious to sustain the honor of a body to which they belong, and in whose confidence and approbation they seek for a high reward, which their sovereign has not to bestow. They sit among the representatives of the nation with a dignity conferred upon them for the public good, not to dictate but to counsel, not to speak with power but to inform with authority. Most conversant with the complicated bearings of the questions brought into consultation, and peculiarly competent to give instruction upon the probable result of the various measures which are proposed, their opinion is seldom heard without compliance, and never without respect. There they confer with the mass of the community, through the medium of their representatives; suggest useful laws, and acquire an intimate acquaintance with the wants, the wishes, and the opinions of the nation. It is their natural and peculiar duty to guard the institutions of the state, which are rarely affected by the speculations of the adventurous innovator, without causing injury to that public whom he intends to court.

In the last parliament holden by King William, the jealousy of the Commons was excessive, and they introduced into the act of settlement, an indiscriminate exclusion of all persons holding any office or place of profit under the King, or receiving any pension from the crown, from serving as members of their house. The restriction, as far as it affected the great officers of state, was instantly found inconvenient and pernicious; and the exclusion was revoked by the Whig Parliament which met in the fourth year of Queen Anne.

The experimental legislators of the national assembly in France, excluded the ministers of their dishonored king from taking place among them. It was their purpose to degrade the royalty, and to arrogate to themselves all honor and power. That exclusion corresponded with their general design. Under that regulation, there was no sympathy among the various departments of the state, no union of counsel, and no co-operation. The ministry was at the mercy of every new cabal; every day calumniated and accused, without the means of justification or defence. When their power was insulted and resisted by a licentious mob, they appeared as supplicants for the ordinary aid of the laws; when the treasury was exhausted, they came down with the humility of beggars; and when their counsel was questioned, and their measures traduced, they stood as vilified and helpless criminals, to apologize for their counsel, to justify their policy, and to implore the forbearance of their presumptuous, ignorant, and mistrustful judges.

The officers of state in the meaner departments, and all persons holding any office created since the accession of Queen Anne, or holding any place or pension at the pleasure of the crown, are excluded from the House of Commons, and even from the elective franchise. Whether the exclusion should be farther extended is a question of policy, to be agitated by the people, when under the pressure of actual grievance, they shall be without hope of redress, through the medium of parliament, owing to the hostile opposition of persons connected with the court. Till then it is a mere matter of expediency, to be considered, like all other matters of legislation, with reference, not only to the evil actually sustained, but also to the benefit of the projected alteration; and it is to be so considered by the legislature itself, and not to be decided by men of speculation; or by those who, unaccustomed to the duties of government, are too powerfully guided by abstract theory, and forget that in balancing the rights of our national orders and degrees, no principle whatever is worthy of respect but on account of the practical advantages to result from its operation. Without the ground of hopeless grievance, the complaint is nugatory and absurd. It is a contention for a phantom of purity, which, in its success, might put to hazard that power of the monarchy, with which the liberties of the people are consolidated, and the energies of the country identified.

It is desired " to curb the pretensions of the " privileged orders so far as that can be effected " without strengthening the royal influence."

In ignorance of any pretensions, inconsistent with law and established usage, advanced by the privileged orders of this country, those who read the Edinburgh Review, with a wish to understand its meaning, must lament, that in this instance at least, their mode of expression is unintelligible. The privileged orders claim no exemption from taxation, justice, or public duty; they exact not the least personal service from the meanest of their fellow subjects; they exercise no precedency in public function, in magistracy, or military command; but they are in absolute equality with all the other orders of the state, in every species of civil right and obligation. What pretensions do they advance which require to be curbed?

Obscurity of expression is not chosen by the learned without design. The reviewers, in this instance, preferred that their meaning should be drawn by ingenious inference, and that their objection to the pretensions of the privileged orders should be understood, as undoubtedly it is intended, to aim at all the privileges of the higher orders.

The Lords, by virtue of their rank, have merely titular distinction. The principal privileges which they claim, equally appertain to the members of the lower house, and they enjoy them as peers of parliament. The Catholic lords, and those who are not peers of parliament, do not claim those privileges.

If the parliamentary trust, dignity, and duties of the upper house be objected to, it is an attack upon " the spirit, as well as the form, of our inva- " luable constitution;" which originally gave precedency of name, and has confirmed an equality of right to the lords, spiritual and temporal.

The authority of that house is less immediately operative in the affairs of state, because it does not rest on the same foundation with that of the commons, who by means of enjoying the exclusive right of proposing taxation, are, in all cases called to concur in the measures of the sovereign, and in extraordinary cases, have been able to controul his counsels. The Lords, with more apparent dignity, are beneficial to the public service in a different respect. They exercise the function of guarding the state from innovation, by their deliberative wisdom. In all ordinary affairs, they readily give sanction to the proceedings of the lower chamber, and have never pertinaciously persisted in opposing any measure which was considered of general utility; but they have it in their power to send back, for further consideration, whatever they disapprove; and thus to prevent the effects of that popular zeal, which might otherwise hastily and indiscreetly give birth to unwise and pernicious laws.

When the Lords of Parliament oppose themselves to any grand proceeding of national polity essentially conducive to the public service; when they oppose their privileges to the common justice of the realm, or shew a disposition to violate those common rights in which, as subjects, they participate, and have an interest to defend; when they are found wanting in their spirit of equity, purity of character, and legislative discretion, which have hitherto been unsuspected, then whatever advantages the sovereign and the people at present derive from their dignity and power, may be renounced in favour of our own more valuable privileges. But while they shall continue beneficially to give weight and example to the proceedings of the lower house; to contribute by their character and influence, in supporting the common justice of the realm, and in manfully defending the common rights, as hitherto they have ever done, without attempting to violate any of them; while in all their deliberations, they shall be found to display an equitable temper, a perfect purity, and a sound discretion, which may moderate the zeal, but cannot be surpassed in degree by the corresponding qualities of the Commons; so long it may be hoped that the people of England will not be jealous of those privileges which are eminently conducive to the dignity, tranquillity, and security of the state.

The personal rank and dignity of a superior order are approved by our constitution, because of their political and moral utility. The Lords are the hereditary representatives of the property of the nation, and give union, permanence, character, weight, and a sort of corporate existence to the whole body of the landed interest. God forbid, in a state which is indebted, above all others, to the successful industry and speculations of commercial adventure, and has derived from its extended traffic, the means of maintaining its power and pre-eminence above the surrounding nations, that the merchant and the manufacturer should be without political consideration. Their encouragement creates and supports a prodigious population, gives life to agriculture, liberally supplies the necessities of government, introduces the splendor of polished life, and affords to the poorest cottager whatever comforts he enjoys. The opulent traders among us, almost exclusively enjoy the honour and advantages of municipal rank, and local magistracy. It will be shewn, in the sequel, how large a portion of parliamentary interest belongs to them. Common observation may prove, that of the influence, power, and precedence, derived from personal opulence and a liberal expenditure, they have a very large proportion. To promote their interests, the legislature readily provides its statutes of encouragement and restriction, of bounty and prohibition, (many of which are of doubtful policy in a view of political economy,)

Complaint has never yet been heard of their being despised or overlooked, or of their wanting an augmentation of influence in the public counsels.

But the landed interest of England, crowned by its hereditary peerage, claims equal regard. The bold peasantry, the virtuous yeomanry, the liberal minded gentry, and the dignified nobles, have interests and feelings distinct, and not less worthy of public care than those of the commercial class. Those interests are peculiarly protected, and those feelings are principally consulted in the upper house of parliament. In that assembly, the projects of the speculative economist are made subservient to the staple interests of the country, and the welfare of the agriculturist and the proprietor, are more naturally protected. There the value of exchanges is more correctly balanced against the sacrifice of dignity and alliance, with which it may be solicited, and the public honour, which none but the slavish and the interested will openly contemn, is there more studiously regarded. There the spirit of the country is least affected by the meaner influence of colonial or commercial views. The love of glory, the pride of national superiority, the affections of generous sentiment, and the disdain of all sordid and selfish consideration in that house, eminently prevail.

The institutions of honour afford to government the means of conferring a cheap, but most envied recompence upon heroic and meritorious character. By the hope of permanent distinction, the heart is stimulated to valour and deeds of noble enterprize. Who shall object to the elevation which his sovereign bestows upon the triumphant warrior, who having overcome the public enemy, is raised, with the concurrence of a grateful country, to permanent pre-eminence? Who shall traduce the rank of the considerate statesman, who having saved the nation by prudent counsel, is called to bear its honours ? Who shall be jealous of the just and learned magistrate, who having faithfully administered the laws in the seat of judgment, is placed in that high tribunal, where his knowledge and example may be more conspicuous, and of more extended benefit ? It is fit that personages of exalted merit should be raised above the commonalty; that their moral distinction may be more illustrious, that others, in the hope of similar advancement, may emulate their virtues; and that they, in an elevated station, may render the most important services to an admiring people.

Far less dignified and useful is any other mode of conferring national reward. The enthusiasm of the heart will not be raised by the hope of pecuniary advantage. Industry, speculation, and labour are well rewarded by that sordid recompence; but contempt of weariness and danger, patience of difficulty, indifference to life, the ardour of enterprize, and that spirit which imparts heroic qualities to every one within its influence and observation, are to be excited and remunerated by different means. Those who are endued with genius and valour, despise the luxuries of wealth, and will not be satisfied with the capricious adulation of a thoughtless multitude; but they will be inspired to achieve whatever is manly, generous, and honorable, by the prospect of that permanent distinction, which will raise them above the sphere of vulgar life, and will descend to their posterity, illustrative of the father's glory, and a motive to emulate his virtues.

The commonalty of England engrossing the power of local magistracy, and by the lower house having a principal weight in the public counsels, and in affairs of legislation, are naturally impressed with greater respect for the wisdom of their representatives by the concurrence of the Lords. It is the temper of a social being to feel deference for the decisions of superiors, and to stand in awe of their judgment, especially when they are known to inquire with candour, and to decide with impartiality. In the proceedings of the Commons, the spirit of party frequently appears, and creates mistrust of the prudence and rectitude of their decisions, in those whose opinions and interests attribute the better argument to the unsuccessful minority. The calmer deliberation and corresponding approbation of the Lords, have a tendency to remove doubt, and to conclude the controversy. Possessing a great mass of property, and having higher interests than those of property to protect, they are able and inclined to reconcile the unprejudiced country resident to that policy, and to those measures of government which they have sanctioned in parliament. In their several counties, they oppose themselves with effect to the discontented caviller, and the shallow objecter. The influence of their estate, rank, and connections is powerful to support those institutions which are conducive to the peace and prosperity of society. The prime object of every social constitution is to make strong and efficient the power of magistracy. Its secondary, but not minor consideration, is to secure against the encroachments of that power, the rights and liberties of the people. In England, we have the royal dignity in which that power is wholly vested with ample prerogative; the privileges of the Commons are also established as a sufficient barrier against the unlawful pretensions of the crown. But the Commons may aim to weaken that prerogative, as probably, and with quite as fatal effect as the crown may attempt to violate those privileges. The institution of the upper house is calculated to guard against either danger. Attached to the sovereign as the fountain of honour, and having no other security than in his supremacy against the hostile jealousy of the Commons, that branch of the legislature is destined to protect the king's power and dignity from impeachment or violation. United to the people by affection, affinity, and common interest, they have always joined in resistance to tyranny and usurpation; and have concurred in every measure necessary to maintain inviolate the public liberties.

The constitution of England, therefore has wisely preserved an hereditary peerage, which, without the means of arrogating to itself oppressive privilege, or of violating the rights, property, or just pretensions of the lower orders, is calculated to give stability, honour, and popularity to the national institutions, to fortify the royal dignity, and to maintain the franchises of the subject.

"A wish to reduce the overgrown influence of " the crown, and to curb the pretensions of the " privileged orders," proceeds in its natural course, " to raise up the power of real talents and worth, " to exalt the mass of the community, and to give " them under the guidance of that virtual aristoc- " racy to direct the counsels of England." The form and the spirit of our constitution, has given to the sovereign exclusively to direct those counsels; subject to the influence and occasional controul of parliament. That wish is altogether subversive of that constitution, which has united in legislation, but not in direct counsel, the royalty, nobility, and national representation; and has placed the mass of the community in subordination and dependence, where its interests will be best promoted, and its influence have due effect; but where it is not admitted to direct or to controul the state.

"The mass of the community" is an expression not much used in political discussion; but having the authority of the Edinburgh Reviewers, it will probably hereafter be current with those of *le peuple souverain*, the majesty of the people, the universal suffrage, and the other expressions used in France, and in the British corresponding societies, from which it varies in form and not in substance. Its meaning is identical with the expressions used as a signal for insurrection, and as a justification of all the excesses which have distinguished the war of the Revolution.

Considering that right of any sort in political application is a matter of substance, and not of form, it is nugatory to refute that abstract right of universal suffrage, which levels its deadly aim at every sort of social institution. Philosophy is a treacherous guide to useful legislation. "*Philo-*"*sophi proponant multa, dictu pulchra, sed ab usu* "*remota.*" It is pregnant with danger to apply any apophthegm, moral or political, to regulate society, without looking to its practical result. The illuminated lodges of the continent were desirous of giving universal prevalence to their disorganizing doctrines, indifferent to the means necessary to that effect, and to the incurable ruin which must follow their ultimate success. Anxious to reduce mankind, by rapid gradations, to that savage independence from which we were rescued, by the introduction of property, laws, and government, they made abstract principle the foundation of their conspiracy, and avowed their contempt of the happiness and prosperity of nations.

The adventurous politician, when he accedes to

abstract principle, without regard to its effects, is little aware to what tremendous consequences he may yield his implied and irrevocable assent. If we admit that the mass of the community is entitled, by natural right, to be raised to politic function, and that the powers of sovereignty are vested in that mass, the process of the principle cannot cease till it disorganizes society. If the mass of the community cannot be bound by a superior authority, because of the natural right of each individual, to concur in making those laws to which he must conform; that right is equally violated when a minority is bound by the will of a greater number. The philosophers, who founded the revolution, perceived that necessary result, and all the awful effects to which it necessarily led. In the excess of their prodigious wickedness, they were bold enough to justify it. "All that we have " done for you hitherto," said the impious Biederman to his besotted pupils, " was only to prepare " you to co-operate in the annihilation of all ma-" gistracy, all governments, all laws, and all civil " society; of every republic, and even democracy, " as well as of every aristocracy or monarchy." " All men are equal and free, this is their impre-" scriptible right, but it is not only under the do-" minion of kings that you are deprived of the ex-" ercise of these rights; they are annulled wher-" ever man recognizes any other law than his own " will." " What right has the people to subject " me and the minority to the decrees of its ma-" jority? Are such the rights of nature? Did " the sovereign or legislative people exist any " more than kings or aristocratic legislators, when " man enjoyed his natural liberty and equality?" " Democratic governments are not more conso-" nant with nature than any others. If you ask

" how it will be possible for men assembled in
" towns, to live in future without laws, magistrates,
" or constituted authorities? The answer is clear.
" Desert your towns and villages, and fire your
" houses. Did men build houses, villages, or
" towns, in the days of the Patriarchs? They were
" all equal and free, the earth belonged to them
" all.". " Their country was the world, and not a
" monarchy or republic in some corner of it."
" Could you but appreciate equality and liberty as
" you ought, you would view with indifference
" Rome, Vienna, Paris, London, or Constantino-
" ple in flames, or any of those towns, boroughs,
" or villages, which you call your country."*

The sagacity of the German philosopher directed him to the ultimate object of the revolutionary principle; his candour disclosed it to the world; his extreme depravity reconciled him to the motive, means, and end, of the vast conspiracy of which it was the original source. But he and all those who adopt any maxim of the system proclaimed by him in final maturity, conceal that fundamental fact of the moral history of mankind, which by imposing the immutable duties of society, abrogated the rights of nature. The solitary inhabitant of the desert, has a right to that savage independence which he may enjoy without dispute, not impaired by any duty which he is required or is able to perform; but confer upon him the common relations of life, those of a father, a child, or a brother, or even that which is necessary for the sustenance and continuation of our kind, and the duties then resulting from the law of nature, conclude that state of independence. The affections,

* Biederman's Critical Inquiry towards the end.
Baurel's Memoirs of Jacobinism. Part iii. Page 262.

of paternal love, filial homage, fraternal regard, and general benevolence, instantly impose the social duties, and the right of personal independence is for ever lost. Those sacred obligations prevail over all the privileges of the wilderness, and give rise to the institutions of society, in the course of property, laws, and government, not upon the basis of natural right, but upon that of natural affection and necessary duty. No abstract doctrine, no contempt of wealth, parentage, kindred, and civil attachment; no traitorous abandonment of the wisdom, virtue, and happiness, resulting from our complicated social character, can justify any one to exclaim with the impious Condorcet—" perish the universe, but may our prin" ciple remain."

The formation of society, which is a law of our nature, not to be abrogated by any process of sophistry or depravity of heart, terminates for ever the rights of natural freedom and equality; in the constitution then to be established, the future benefit of mankind, and not the abrogated abstract right is to be exclusively regarded. " In jure non " remota causa sed proxima spectatur."

To form a correct judgment of our political institutions, we are to keep exclusively in view, the end for which they exist, and that end is the virtue, happiness, and security of the state. "Finis " enim et scopus, quem leges intueri atque ad " quem Jussiones et Sanctiones suas dirigere debent " non alius est, quam ut cives feliciter degant: id " fiet, si pietate et religione recte instituti; mori" bus honesti; armis adversus hostes externos tuti; " legum auxilio adversus seditiones et privatas inju" rias muniti; imperiis et magistratibus obsequentes; " copiis et opibus locupletes et florentes fuerint. " Harum autem rerum instrumenta et nervi sunt

" leges." * We ought to be gratefully content, if by the constitution of our House of Commons, from which our legislation principally flows, the purpose for which it ought to exist has completely been attained, and is not yet found to fail: if our citizens live happily, religiously, morally, secure from foreign hostility, domestic sedition, and private injury, obedient to the laws and magistrates, opulent and flourishing.

That we may long enjoy these advantages of government, that house was endued with its legislative function; that it may answer the end of its institution, it is a delegation from the whole nation, with respect to estate, municipal privilege, commercial opulence, and popular interest. It comprises an adequate representation of whatever might want legislative care, or be fitted to express national opinion. It is not necessary that the suffrage of every individual, should be given to depute his own representative. The minority on the poll at a contested election, are effectually represented by the successful candidate, who when elected, is not the exclusive representative of his immediate constituents, but is a member of that assembly, which constitutionally and collectively represents the whole British nation.

Whether or not the elective franchise is too strictly limited, and ought to be extended, is a question of expediency, and not of right. In the latter view it has no claim to any, in the other it requires but little consideration.

As on the one side, the limitation of it to proprietors of estate, would give to the landed interest an undivided and uncontrouled power, so on the other an illimitable extension of it to every house-

* Bacon de Justitia Universali sive de fontibus Juris.

holder, would deprive property of its necessary weight, and expose us to the uncertain and improvident influence of the multitude and the mob. If the elective corporations were laid open the commercial class might want an adequate influence, and by a disfranchisement of the Boroughs, the gross population might be deprived of all share in counsel. But the franchise being variously distributed, every prevailing interest has its just weight in the representation, and with the checks and powers provided in the other branches of the legislature, a beautiful harmony is secured, such as never elsewhere belonged to a balanced and free constitution. The counties depute their members to represent the landed property, and permanent local interests; the corporations delegate those who express the wants and wishes of traders and manufacturers; the boroughs and the great towns, select the men of talents, and the candidates for popular fame; and the universities, are admitted to send a very small number, peculiarly expected to watch over the interests of learning and the church.

The patronage of boroughs, and the corruption of electors, occasion censure and complaint. As immoral, censure cannot be too loud; as illegal, punishment cannot be too severe, when such abuses are detected; for they lead to a breach of the most sacred obligations. But the extent of the evil is much less than the enemies of the constitution assert, and in the degree in which it exists, its effect is very different from what they assume. The appropriated boroughs are not found to give a dangerous preponderance to the families which enjoy that patronage; from the correction of that evil, a greater might ensue, in the reduction of the terest of the fixed property of the country, which rather requires augmentation. By the corruption of the electors, the men of acquired wealth and mere personal consideration, have an access to Parliament, where some of them ought to be, but to which they would not so probably come, by a mode of election altogether pure.

Theoretical defect in this instance, as in many others, is practical perfection. In vain would speculators devise a plan of election to afford advantages, similar to those derived from the varied rights and customs of franchised places. By no other means could we bring into union and co-operation a great body of legislators, whose interests, opinions, and prejudices, are those of every description of people, composing the body politic, some of whom are jealously alert to defend their particular order from the minutest inequality of public burthen, and all of whom from a conviction of individual weakness, are watchful of their common liberties. By persevering in that course which our ancestors ran before us, we may retain the prize of practical liberty: by yielding to the illusion of parliamentary reform, we may like Atalanta be deprived of our substantial object, in stooping for a golden bauble.

"nitidique cupidine pomi
"Declinat cursus; aurumque volubile tollit.

The House of Commons, practically, is an assembly, not only legislative in conjunction with the other estates, in which capacity it is truly representative of the people, but is also, with respect to the ordinary affairs of government, mediative between the subject and the prince, in which character, having a power irresistible by either party, it ought in degree to be representative both of the crown and the nation. That latter faculty it acquired incidentally from the pecuniary dependence of government upon the contributions of the commonalty, and though it is not strictly conformable with our original constitution, its operation has been beneficial in the highest degree. Its beneficial operation commenced with that period when contention between the people and the sovereign was happily concluded, and the executive government was admitted indirectly to join in the deliberations, and to have some weight in the decisions of parliament. Necessarily controuled by the wisdom of the legislature, it is now permitted by means of its proper advocates, sometimes, to instruct that wisdom, and always to prevent precipitancy of decision. If by the entire exclusion of all persons connected with the state, no other voice but that of the people could be heard in the lower house; a great and injurious change would ensue in our practical constitution. The people would then acquire an absolute supremacy, to be exercised so long as it might endure, without check or responsibility. Their claims, however inordinate, in all measures of government, foreign and domestic, would not be stated as admonitory counsel or solicitation, but would be imperiously advanced to awe and to decide; and the monarchy, if it could subsist in any form conjunctively with such democratic domination, must subsist in subjection to its dictates, opinions, and caprices.

The House of Commons now bears the proclaimed censure of a very large portion of the people, occasioned by the result of a late important inquiry, unfavourable to the wishes, and opposed to the principles of those who are most active in procuring that censure. The original promc lic approbation, in a manner which casts reflection on the whole representative body, and the several minorities who voted in opposition to the propositions of ministers on that occasion participate in such approbation. What were the motives of that honourable commoner in bringing forward his accusations against this illustrious personage; and what was the force of the evidence adduced in support of it, however important for the consideration of the multitudes who now oppose the sense of parliament, expressed with regard to that evidence, will not here be discussed. Such opposition may be directed, by designing men, to objects infinitely more important than the character of the distinguished commoner, or of the high functionary whom he has stigmatized, or even of that tribunal which decided the case upon full and laborious consideration. The question is already raised into permanent national importance: it is involved with the matter of parliamentary reform now asserted to be evidently necessary; it is adduced as conclusive proof of a system of corruption, loathsome and universal; and in its tendency it threatens to alienate the confidence of the people from their legislative rulers.

If the whole mass of accusation brought into parliament against the Royal Duke were admitted to be true, though the evidence adduced in support of it certainly did not establish the half of that accusation; or, if implicit credit be given to the whole of that evidence, informal, insufficient, and inconclusive as it was, there would yet be wanting ground to maintain the illimitable effects which some men derive from it. Such admission, however it might inculpate the Duke of York, would not establish as a fact, even that his military administration was altogether corrupt. It could be tortured no farther than to prove that, in the several cases mentioned in the accusation, respect had been paid in ten or twelve instances of patronage and official regulation, to the venal recommendation of a mistress.

"The very head and front of his offending
"Hath this extent: no more."

If the number of those cases were gratuitously ten times multiplied, the concession would not amount to the alleged result, nor would it warrant an inference that an hundredth part of the patronage of the army was tainted by that corruption. Nor by any possibility of fair inference would it warrant a suspicion that such corruption extended to any other servant of the state. Rigorous justice might, indeed, exact that the royal Duke should no longer retain his high employment; the virtue of those who fill high official situations, should be, like that of Cæsar's wife, above suspicion; but that end being accomplished by his resignation, nothing remains in the whole mass of accusation to affect the character of government.

Such admission may lead to one farther consequence, affecting the decision of a majority of the lower house of parliament, which, though not strictly corresponding with the tenor of the evidence, might be ground of inculpation against them. But it is unworthy of this generous nation to judge harshly of their representatives in a matter of such extreme delicacy and importance. The royal Duke had been pursued unrelentingly to disgrace; and the event has proved that, however he might be clear, in conscience, of not meriting such disgrace, yet he could not be sheltered from it by authority, influence, or prerogative. It was no longer possible for him under the odium attached to his ministration to retain the exercise of power. He solemnly declared his innocence, and obtained a formal exculpation, but nevertheless yielding to the ascertained judgment of the country, without admitting its correctness, he withdrew from an appointment which he could no longer hold with unsuspected honour. Is parliament to be censured, in this case, for not pursuing their victim in defiance of all forms of law, all rules of evidence, and all principles of equity, to absolute destruction? For having some respect to the feelings of a beloved sovereign, and to that fond personal attachment to the royal house, which the nation, their constituents, have so often professed at the foot of the throne? For feeling some reluctance to enter upon their journals, an indelible accusation of infamy against him who is so near the throne, and may eventually fill it; and for declining to drag him as a culprit, under circumstances which at least were doubtful, before a tribunal of justice, there to vindicate his character, confronted with a shameless harlot? The House of Commons in its accusative capacity does not strictly exercise a representative function, but is to discharge a judicial duty, tempered by sound political consideration. Though the effervescence occasioned by a proceeding so extraordinary as yet prevents a calm consideration of the motives which justify the decision of parliament, and there are those who artfully direct the public eye to a partial view of it, yet the day may come when an undivided people shall consider that the national vengeance has been sufficiently severe, and that any further measure which might lower the dignity of royalty itself, and shake the main pillar of the constitution, would be perilous and unwise, not required by justice, rejected by generosity, and hoped for only by those who extend their view very far beyond the punishment of such guilt, as that imputed to the Duke of York.

A great part of the majority in parliament, upon that interesting question, is accused of voting under the influence of appointment, place, or pension, or of connection with those who have them; and every one supposed subject to such influence being excluded from that list of the votes, it is alleged that the present minority would have obtained the decision by a surplus of eight or nine votes. Are we to admit that all persons enjoying the bounty of the crown, and voting with ministers, are corruptly influenced by that bounty, while in the ranks of opposition we see many who have enjoyed the liberal favour of their sovereign, and who shewed little reluctance to cast censure upon the royal Duke? May we not also doubt whether in those ranks there were none but patriots as pure and undaunted as Mr. Wardle is supposed to be? May not some be found there, who supported him under the influence of the love of popularity, or of the hope of personal advancement in the series of prodigious events which may now commence. It betrays a beggarly ignorance of the human heart to believe that all the opponents of illustrious station are of perfect integrity and patriotism, and at the same time to charge all those who derive any benefit from the patronage of their king with always acting in selfish consideration of that benefit, without any sense of justice, honour, or propriety.

What new reasons for a reform of parliament arise out of this case, viewed in the light in which generosity and justice place it, faction itself cannot allege. If corruption had crept into the office of the Commander in Chief, it has been the effect of the late proceedings to root it out. The proceedings of the legislature in the course of that inquiry were unawed by power, and its decision was the most deliberate which any popular assembly ever made. That legislature is busily employed to search out every abuse, in every part of the public administration, and shews a disposition, honestly and effectually, to cure it. What more can be expected from any description of parliament. Attached to the constitution, not for its vices, but for its excellencies, let us hope that the clamour for reform, now excited by those who for twenty years have eulogized revolutions and censured all the measures of government, may speedily subside in good sense and generous loyalty; and that as little may now be accomplished by those who would sacrifice substantial benefit to theoretical amendment as in former times, when the country sought and found its safety in other measures, and from other counsellors.

In England there is a power of popular opinion, which has at all times controuled the policy of government, and the counsels of the legislature, and affords an ample security for the public liberties. Europe cannot boast of the existence of that power excepting in the British Isles. In all her other states, she languishes under a ferocious despotism, which exacts implicit obedience and slavish adulation, to a stern and low born conqueror. It is England alone, illustriously seated upon her unshaken rocks, which yet retains the antique flame of liberty, to be regulated but not repressed by reason and by law; a flame which can never be extinguished while it draws its supply from popular opinion.

The force of that opinion will never suffer the rights of the subject to be violated or impaired by any parliament or prince. That would be its wise and constitutional application, but such is its irresistible power, that in many instances it has operated even in opposition to the sounder policy of government. The inadequate stipulations of the peace of Utrecht, which gave rise to subsequent desolating wars, and to the present preponderance of France, were made in compliance with that opinion. The impolitic war with Spain in 1739, in obvious opposition to the wisdom of ministers, and the true interests of the empire was occasioned by that opinion. In the peace of 1763, the advantages of our most successful and glorious warfare in the four quarters of the globe, were conceded to the same operating cause. The peace of 1782, and that which suspended for a short period the present eventful contest, were also produced by an application of the same power. When the people of England raise their voice in clamorous petition and remonstrance, the power of parliament itself is compelled to yield its better judgment, and the prerogative of the crown is abandoned to the demand of popular opinion.

The great Roman statesman pronounced the form of the British constitution, to surpass in excellence, whatever else could be devised. "Statuo "esse optime constitutam Rempublicam quæ ex "tribus generibus illis, regali, optimo, et populari, "modicè confusa."* Tacitus adopted his opinion, but having surveyed the various governments of nations, and considered the nature of the human heart, in its essential principles and temper, unchangeable in time or place, he thought that the mixed government of England, was rather a creature of imagination than a political possibility; and

* Ciceronis Fragmenta.

that if it could be established by a fortunate and unlooked-for concurrence of circumstances, it must be of short duration. " Cunctas nationes et " urbes, populus, aut priores, aut singuli regunt. " Delecta ex his et constituta reipublicæ forma, " laudari facilius quam evenire ; vel si evenit, haud " diuturna esse potest."* But many centuries have rolled away since this nation began to flourish under that form of government. It yet flourishes under that form, because a destructive collision of the opposing powers is practically prevented, without impairing that actual balance from which the excellence of the institution results.

If the features of the British constitution have been faithfully, though hastily delineated, in these observations, can the upright sentiment of the candid inquirer dissent from that judgment which has hitherto prevailed in all countries, of the unrivalled excellence of our government, and the practical perfection of our liberties. If under that government those liberties have been matured, while the nation has uniformly advanced in power and dignity, and now stands unequalled in glory, arts, and commerce, defying the hostility of a confederated world, and majestically serene during those convulsions, which subvert the surrounding states ; how guilty are those conspirators, who by calumny and falsehood asperse the character, and vilify the conduct of that sage and patriotic institution ! What horror and indignation perturb the British heart, while the atrocious libellers continually invite us to "change radical reform and revolution."

The apostacy of Mr. Cobbett and the Edinburgh Reviewers, is an aggravation of their crime.

* Tacit. Ann. lib. iv.

Theirs is not the sin of ignorance. The early publications of the Political Register, displayed sentiments of general loyalty ; and were calculated to appease the threatening storm of jacobinism in this happy country. Mr. Cobbett had abandoned that honourable course, and was the avowed advocate of revolution, when the reviewers justly censured his infamous attacks upon all our social establishments. They told us only eighteen months ago, "That there was such a vast overbalance of
"good in our situation, as was well worth a strug-
"gle to preserve, and that revolution or conquest
"were to be regarded with the utmost abhorrence
"and dismay." They assured us "that we had
"attained a greater portion of happiness than had
"ever before been enjoyed by any other nation ;
"and that the frame and administration of our
"polity, was the most perfect and beneficial of
"any that men had yet invented and reduced to
"practice." "That as the good which we already
"have, greatly exceeds that of which we imagine
"we are deprived, it would be in the highest
"degree criminal and imprudent to expose it to
"any considerable hazard, for the desperate chance
"of increasing it by the uncertain issue of a revo-
"lution." Admitting the complaints of venal electors, and a parliament subject to the influence of the crown, they stated "that so far from being of
"opinion, that the alteration of those parts of our
"system would cure this or any other evil, they
"were persuaded that such a measure would have
"a contrary effect." They asserted that "in point
"of fact, the parliament actually possessed the re-
"quisites on which its substantial value depends."
They thought that "a certain infusion of the
"influence of the crown and peers, in the House
"of Commons, was essential to the existence of

" our mixed government," and, " that the exclu-
" sion from the parliament of the official advisers
" of the sovereign, would degrade the legislature,
" without purifying it in the smallest degree."
They considered it " mere faction, to say that the
" sinecure places and pensions, or the sums lost
" by speculation, made any sensible addition to
" the burthens of the nation." They expressed
" their indignation at Mr. Cobbett's schemes of
" reform, and at his attempts to weaken the respect
" and attachment of the people to forms and esta-
" blishments, without which there would be no
" security for their freedom." " From a revolution
" they could then anticipate little but general de-
" gradation and misery."

Such were the sentiments of the Edinburgh Reviewers, eighteen months ago. Such sentiments they had not hastily adopted, nor did they then for the first time announce them. In April, 1805, they told us that " our House of Commons is made up," as they said it ought to be, " by the individuals, who by birth, fortune, or talents, possess singly the greatest influence over the rest of the people." *
Their present outcry is for change, radical reform, and revolution: the same with that still raised by Mr. Cobbett. May the British nation, indignant at their shameless apostacy, and too wise to abandon at their suggestion, the beneficent institutions of our forefathers, with one voice reply to their treacherous counsel like the Earls and Barons of King Henry's time, " quod nolunt leges Angliæ " mutare quæ usitatæ sunt et approbatæ." May we still be tranquil and prosperous under the government of a patriotic monarch, and cherish those invaluable liberties, which are ascertained and protected by the law.

* See their Review of the " Memoires de Bailly."

END OF PART III.

THE
RIGHTS
OF THE
SOVEREIGNTY.

PART THE FOURTH.

THE moral revolution in Europe was complete long before there was any appearance of political convulsion. The men of letters, as writers of history and fable, of poetry and romance, of philosophy and science, of religion and rational research, had effected an important change in the opinions, manners, and prejudices of mankind. Their co-operation, during a long time, was without confederacy, but nevertheless they were severally employed in the pursuit of the common object, and by their incessant activity and varied ingenuity, they constituted at an early period, that vast conspiracy which now triumphs in the overthrow of thrones, the subversion of morals, and the inefficiency of religious restraint.

At the commencement of those political convulsions, which have desolated Europe, and prostrated so many states; which have subjected mighty nations to the revolutionary sword, and given to France a preponderance hardly desired, and never anticipated by her most ambitious kings; there were in this country two parties, the one bold, militant, and conspiring, which aimed at subverting the government and causing a revolution; similar in principle and object to that which then raged upon the continent; the other timid, hardly conscious of the danger, and disposed to be quiescent. It wished rather to evade a contest, than to crush the hostility threatened by its presumptuous enemy.

Those who at that period conducted the affairs of England, were attached to the spirit of liberty; natural to their countrymen, and did not readily perceive that the licentiousness of France had a different origin and temper. Mr. Pitt had been nursed in the whig principles of this country. In infancy he had been taught to admire, and to cherish those popular rights which are engrafted in the British constitution. The popularity of his great name, was augmented by his early and continued efforts in vindication of those rights. Even in office he had been a strenuous advocate of parliamentary reform, and was justly esteemed an able and sincere supporter of that freedom, which Englishmen regard as their boast and birthright. From habit, principle, character, and interest, he was a friend to general liberty, and certainly was not the first to feel indignation, at the excesses of the insurgents in France. When fatal experience had given irresistible proof of the malignity of the new doctrines, even then he did not estimate the extent of the threatening peril. Wedded to his pacific system, he reluctantly abandoned it when imperious circumstances dictated a different policy.

Mr. Pitt was devoted to maintain the established peace, that his sinking fund, and other schemes of economy, might have a permanent operation, and that the flourishing commerce, and extended resources of the country, might still progressively increase. When the war had actually broken out in Europe, he refused to unite with the Emperor and the King of Prussia. In the spring of 1792, he made a reduction of the military and naval establishments, and discontinued the subsidy of alliance, paid to the Landgrave of Hesse. On the 21st of February, he expressed in parliament his expectation, that the peace would continue at least fifteen years. In May, a proclamation was issued prohibiting all persons from accepting letters of service from the enemies of France, which the French government acknowledged as an evidence " of the sentiments of humanity, justice, and peace, " at that time manifested by his Britannic Ma- " jesty;" and at the prorogation of parliament in June, the king " expressed his confidence of pre- " serving to his people the uninterrupted blessings " of peace.

That pacific conduct on the part of this country was pursued, when the proceedings of the National Assembly in France had already assumed a character incompatible with the safety of society. The philosophers of this country had hailed the revolution as the day-star of liberty;* the British constitution was already reprobated as an institution of tyranny, corruption, and oppression. Affiliated societies were established to confederate with France, and to apply among ourselves the doctrine of universal insurrection. An outcry was begun " for change, radical reform, and revolu- " tion."

It is upon indelible record, that the ministers of this country were driven from their pacific system, by the violence and the direct aggression of the revolutionary power, then directing the affairs of France. The war of defence which Mr. Pitt was compelled to undertake, then saved the state; and the object of the conspiracy was for a time defeated.

But the restless spirit of jacobinism when crushed, is not subdued; checked, but not overcome by the vigour of Mr. Pitt's administration, it yet lives and labors in its unalterable purpose. It yet struggles for pre-eminence, it has abandoned none of its original pretensions, it still adheres to its abstract principles of anarchy, and its means are the same with those originally adopted in the conspiracy.

The conspirators in this country are still active in promulgating the delusive, execrable doctrine of the Rights of Man, to justify rebellion. Many of them, and among them the Edinburgh Reviewers, attempt to weaken the national resentment against the enemy, by applauding the policy and conduct of France, during the war of the revolution, and by censure and condemnation of the allies. The operations of our warfare they stigmatize and oppose; the domestic policy of government, they asperse and vilify. Persons of the highest rank they indiscriminately accuse, calumniate, and traduce. They complain of the restraints of the law upon outrageous libellers, as violations of the liberty of the press; and in all their proceedings they provoke the most malignant passions of the lowest classes, and would incite them to discontent, disaffection, and outrage.

The Edinburgh Reviewers commenced their discussion of Spanish affairs, by asserting dogmatically, " that France was not always the aggressor " in any point of view. For example, the first " coalition against the revolution was a manifest " war of aggression on the part of the allies." " The blame which men always attach to the party " who first breaks the peace, fell constantly upon " the enemies of France; and it did so happen " that her conduct at the treaties which generally " followed these disastrous campaigns, was suffi-

"ciently moderate, considering her enormous
"victories, to keep up the same impression.
"Every thing bore the appearance of France
"being forced into hostilities, by the jealousy,
"the fears, or the restlessness of her neighbours,
"acting under the influence of England; having
"been compelled to beat them from one end of
"Europe to the other; and then taking as little as
"she well could of their territory, as a punish-
"ment for their past aggressions, and a security
"for their keeping the peace in future."

Those bold assertions, made at a time when France was insolently sporting with the fragments of the powerful countries which coalesced in the first alliance, and when the great monarchs of Europe, plundered, oppressed, and enchained by their triumphant foe, seemed to retain no other hope or consolation, than that derived from the justice of their cause, were a harsh and uncharitable judgment. At every former period, when the English nation sympathized with all the misfortunes which strength could inflict upon the weak, and placed itself as if impelled by its generous nature, in hatred and opposition to every proud oppressor, such a statement would have been regarded as a cruel mockery of the afflicted, and an insult to suffering merit. Two hundred years ago, the case of the elector Palatine, the relative and ally of King James, to whom alone he could look for succour in his extreme calamity, was not scrutinized so strictly. When the magnanimous resolution of Maria Theresa was almost the only hope of her subjects, against that torrent of hostility which threatened to overwhelm them, and when the King of Prussia in the next war, was reduced to a lower state of weakness and necessity, the English nation in either case, would not have tolerated a doubt, far less an unqualified condemnation of the justice of those potentates, whose safety was to result from our cordial friendship and assistance. To compassionate the fate, and to aid the efforts of those whom any tyranny would bind in fetters, and to curb the insolent boasting of any usurpation, were formerly not only the policy of our government, but the generous and enthusiastic desire of our undivided people. Those whose arguments would maintain the haughty conqueror in his scheme of aggrandizement, approve the pretences of his warfare, and take no sympathy with the subjugated states which fell beneath his sword, were little likely to meet with the applause and acquiescence of the British public.

If the time approaches when the suffering nations, following the example of Spain, will be roused by the spirit of loyalty and patriotism, to drive away the creatures of despotism, whom the great usurper has elevated to rule them; in that case, this country must not consider their present humiliation "as a punishment for their past ag-"gressions." Our people will be slow to institute that process of inquiry and crimination, which raises the enemy of England to be a dispenser of national justice, and sanctifies the violence and treachery, which render him the arbiter of Europe. We remain unconquered and undismayed. Rather than by an uncalled for judgment, to break the hopes of those, who may at this instant with anxious desire require our help, to contend again with the hordes of the tyrant, and to regain their independence, let our mind be impressed with a conviction, that their bondage originated in the unprovoked aggression of an implacable foe, whose great acquirements, must in justice be restored to their rightful possessors, and whose power must be balanced and restrained within reasonable limits, before we can expect or hope to extinguish the torch of war, or to have security against his unbounded ambition.

The justice of the cause of the allies might at one time have been obscured by the passions and prejudices of men; but now the narration of the circumstances in which that war originated, is clear and unequivocal. History and philosophy have pronounced their joint arbitration upon the important question, and no one assuming to himself a dictatorial function superior to the councils of his sovereign, and the unanimous protestations of faithful co-operation made by our loyal nation at the commencement of that eventful contest, not yet concluded, can pronounce that the war was "a manifest war of aggression on the part "of the allies," but in absolute opposition to truth and reason.

It was the habitual policy of all the founders of the revolution to pursue their project without ever yielding to the proofs or the reasoning of their opponents. The demonstration of innocence or merit, was no shield against their calumnies and enmity. The authority of truth, in refutation of their speculations, never reduced them to silence and submission. Those who adopt their speculations and labour in the same cause, by the same means of seditious argument and false narration, will argue in defiance of conviction and narrate in opposition to established fact.

The question of the war of the revolution, cannot now be advanced as a matter of curiosity, or historic doubt; it is moved, and pertinaciously retained, because it involves the most important matters that can interest mankind. As a question of fact, it is equally important with any other matter of authentic history: with patient investigation and perfect ment in that view of the subject. There is another view in which, impelled by every national interest, and every moral obligation, we become indifferent even to the results of historic inquiry, as they are limited only to a scientific purpose. When we perceive that the established law of Europe in the balance of the respective powers, for the order and the security of the whole was then contested; that the legal bond which united men in social relation, was then disputed; and that every fundamental maxim of magistracy was in violent litigation, it becomes a more imperious duty to weigh that question with the utmost force of our reasoning faculties, and the most extended scope of free inquiry. It is not then our duty to inquire with impartiality, because he who is impartial upon that subject is already of corrupted judgment, and in effect has decided favourably to the regicides of France.

Hostilities commmenced in Europe in April, 1792, when the National Assembly declared war against the King of Hungary and Bohemia.

At the formation of the National Assembly, France was at peace with the whole world; bound in many federal relations by which her ambition ought to have been restrained, while her interests and dignity were promoted. Austria, her antient military rival, united to her by close family alliance, had reposed so firmly in the solidity of her friendship, that the iron frontier of the Netherlands was dismantled, and the country exposed to all her incursions. In the empire she still maintained her accustomed preponderance, and was regarded as the natural protector of the protestant league. England, her most formidable opponent, humbled in the war of the American emancipation, and weakened by the struggles of domestic faction, which were occasioned by that contest, had shewn a determination to persevere in a system of policy the most pacific, and was already bound to her by intimate ties of friendship. Spain was her ready coadjutor in war and negotiation, and held the resources of her opulence and her vast empire, to promote her views, and succour her pretensions. The princes of Italy were busily employed in plans of legislative regulation, to ameliorate the condition of their subjects, to improve their fiscal institutions, and territorial riches. The Dutch republic, harassed by an improvident contest with England, their natural ally, and by the civil intrigues for power, between the Stadtholder and the States, was disposed to pursue in peace their commercial speculations, and to repair the disastrous effects of their recent impolicy. The whole of the European confederacy was animated by one universal disposition to improve their established relations in perfect amity, and to pursue the first duty of sovereigns, in providing for the happiness and prosperity of the people, uninterrupted by the clamours of war, and not diverted from that beneficent policy by projects of ambition and vain glory.

The monarchy of France, though less solicitous of that foreign domination, to which its former sovereigns had aspired, was nevertheless far more prosperous, and apparently rested on more solid foundations than at any earlier period. With respect to its martial array, both military and maritime, it was secure from danger, superior to insult, and fearless of attack. The government with all its faults and defects, (for what human institution is without faults and defects!) was well suited to the natural disposition of the French people. The king was exceedingly beloved, and his personal prerogative not unpopular. All the powers of the state had shewn a prevailing inclination to remedy, even by great sacrifices, whatever abuses had been occasioned by the ignorance of a darker period, or the corruption naturally incident to all great establishments. Property was protected by the laws; personal liberty was rarely violated by prerogative, and might be said to be sacred and inviolate, and freedom of religious opinion, though not absolutely legal, was practically tolerated. The courts of justice were filled by enlightened magistrates, whose decisions are at this day respected, even in the tribunals of this country; they were far above the controul of power, and entirely unsuspected of venality, or a slavish respect to any species of authority. The commerce of the great towns, sustained by an industrious and increasing population, had given life to a flourishing agriculture, and to all manner of useful speculations. The political structure of that great community, seemed to be fixed on deep foundations; its various arrangements were calculated for the dignity and decent accommodation of all the classes, which constitute a well ordered society, while no proof was wanting, that the state and all its orders were in an ameliorated and improving condition. To the merely political observer, that government shewed no symptom of weakness or decay. Its finances indeed had fallen into disorder, but they were not dilapidated. It felt the pernicious effects of past improvidence, which economy of expence might speedily have cured, or a prudent management of receipt might have removed. But its ministers were of the school of the Experimental Philosophy, and made the necessities of the state, the means of giving birth to their beloved child of promise, generated in the excesses of vanity and licentiousness. Though the boundless prodigality of the succeeding powers, has shewn what vast resources might have been commanded by the monarchy, wisely and vigourously administered, yet those treacherous speculators would exert none of the legal energies, which belonged to the sovereign for his constitutional support, but hastened to place him in dependence upon the third chamber of the states general of the kingdom.

The monarchy, in temper and interest, was become entirely pacific. The National Assembly was a power hitherto unknown in Europe, created to acquire a new interest in war and in public commotion; naturally of a temper to pursue all its projects, indifferent to all the consequences which they might eventually occasion.

The first principle which was adopted by the National Assembly, was to make itself a sovereign revolutionary power, which annulled every species of authority and jurisdiction appurtenant to the established government, and created for itself an unexampled supremacy, equally inconsistent with all the domestic institutions, and all the foreign relations of France. In the abolition of all ecclesiastical and territorial rights, they had comprehended those of the German States, in Alsace, Franche Comté and Loraine, and the other provinces ceded to Louis the Fourteenth; though those rights had been solemnly confirmed by the peace of Westphalia, and by every subsequent treaty between France and the Empire, and had been respected amidst all the wars which had agitated Europe. This positive violation of treaties, and unprecedented attack upon independent states, occasioned a series of complaints from the Emperor and the Germanic Diet. On the part of France, the assembly absolutely refused to abrogate their unjust proceedings, or to give satisfaction for the injury committed, and voted a great augmentation of the military force.

At this conjuncture of affairs, the forcible occupation of Avignon convinced the world, that the French government were meditating a more dangerous system of encroachment and hostility, than that which had formerly threatened the independence of the empire and of Europe. But the emperor dreaded to involve himself in the horrors of war, from which he had recently delivered his country, and raised the wonder of all Europe, by his anxiety to remove every pretext for attack. He withdrew his troops from the French frontier, reduced his army, and laboured to allay the ferment excited in the Diet, by the injustice of the National Assembly.*

It is most important here to remember, that whatever questions were yet in discussion, between the Germanic empire and the new revolutionary power, they were purely occasioned by the direct aggressions of France on the rights of those independent princes, and were wholly unconnected with any consideration of the antisocial principles, already developed in the proceedings of the National Assembly. The emigration of the loyal and persecuted nobility and proprietors, of that lacerated and disjointed commonwealth, had yet scarcely begun; no standard was yet raised, round which the exiled and virtuous gentry might rally to redeem their country; nor had any potentate whatever, imagined the necessity of opposing the revolutionary torrent, by that resistance which was adopted unhappily at too late a period.

New and decided proofs of hostility were displayed by the ruling power in France. The preliminaries of a defensive alliance were concluded in July 1791, between the Emperor and the King of Prussia, with a view to unite the other great

* Coxe's House of Austria.

monarchies, in a plan for their general safety. In August was issued the declaration of Pilnitz, general and unspecific, which led to no important consequences.* On the acceptance of the constitution by Louis the Sixteenth, the emperor formally acknowledged the validity of the revolution, received the French ambassador, revoked his circular letter to the sovereigns of Europe, and admitted the revolutionary flag into his ports; he rejected all plans of hostile aggression, received with coolness the expostulations of the empress Catharine, and scarcely deigned to listen to the chivalrous projects of the King of Sweden.

A series of insults and provocations, and a systematic plan of hostility were pursued on the part of France. New subjects for invective were discovered by the Brissotines, and new pretences devised for precipitating the nation into that conflict, to which they looked forward as the means of establishing their darling republic, and extending the empire of their baleful principles. The king was swept away by the torrent. The revolution triumphed over all opposition: no language of moderation, or complaint of calumny, made by the emperor, could avert the calamities of the

---

* "Déférant, pour la forme, á la sensibilité, aux instances "importúnes des freres de Louis XVI, l'Empereur et le Roi de "Prusse, signèrent cette convention insignifiante et superflue, "dont les dernières démarches du Roi de France * faisoient "tomber l'objet. Contens de cette démonstration d'intérêt, "que les refugies se hâtèrent de répandre comme un mani- "festa décisif, les deux souverains se replièrent in continent "sur leur précédente neutralité : pas un de leurs soldats ne s'é- "branla ; la constitution reçue par la Roi de France, au sortir "de sa prison et sous peine du détrônement, paralysa cet ac- "cord de Pilnitz, que les politiques ont rangé dans la classe des "comédies augustes." Mercure Hist. et pol. Janvier 1792.

* The acceptance and proclamation of the new constitution of Louis the Sixteenth

projected war. The terrific tumult every day acquired new violence, till at length the National Assembly, with only seven dissenting voices, amidst the plaudits of a senseless and debased multitude, decreed war against the King of Hungary and Bohemia.*

The Brissotines, who then decided the councils of France, were not willing to lose the reputation of wholly provoking the contest, nor did they pretend that it was a manifest war of aggression on the part of the allies. Their object was to be obtained by offensive hostility against the sovereigns of Europe, and they never dreamt of forbearance in that vast project of their ambition. In October, 1791, Brissot exclaimed in the assembly, "il ne faut pas vous défendre; il faut attaquer "vous même." In December, he exclaimed "la "guerre est actuellement un bienfait national, et "la seule calamité qu'il y ait à redouter, c'est de "n'avoir pas la guerre." Legendre said, "la liberté "doit rouler les tyrans dans la poussière, et fouler "les trônes qui ont écrasé le monde." In January, Brissot announced, "une guerre est indispensable "pour consommer la revolution, voici le moment "ou nous allons publier la guerre." "Il faut

* Apology is due for introducing matter known to all Europe, but if falsehood be a thousand times advanced with the confidence of established truth, it will be necessary a thousand times to refute it. The above relation is partly drawn from Coxe's History of the House of Austria, the only work yet published in this country which brings narrative with the dignity and correctness of history to the establishment of the French republic. That Historian justly appreciates his reputation for candour and authenticity, and has closed his work when he found it impossible "to compile from imperfect documents, and amidst the "misrepresentations of passion and prejudice, a faithful account "of those portentous revolutions which have totally changed "the political relations and importance of Austria, and con- "founded all the antient connexions of Europe." *Preface to his history of the House of Austria.*

"rompre avec tous les cabinets," said Cambon. "Il faut incendier les quatre coins de l'Europe :— "notre salut est la," said Brissot to his constituents. If direct proof of their hostile determination, were not abundantly supplied by their own positive declarations, too numerous and too frequent to admit of doubt or misconstruction, the whole scheme of their revolution is decisive of the fact. The war was the necessary result of their policy, their free and natural choice, and their own unprovoked aggression.*

Although the crime of actual aggression had been doubtful with respect to France, yet the allies would have been justified by the law of nations, by the force of treaties incorporated into that law, by the precedents of other times, and the natural rights of self preservation, for a hostile interference to overcome by force, when it might have been overcome, an aspiring power whose existence was incompatible with their safety. They ought not to have waited till that power was matured and able to execute his destructive purpose. The whelp of the lion is not to be spared, because as yet he has not sallied from his mother's den. Happy had it been for mankind, if the great sovereigns of Europe, had sooner mistrusted the canting and false professions of the first rebels, against lawful authority in France. The revolutionary monster came into being without fair natural pro-

---

* The statements of the Rev. Herbert Marsh, in "his History "of the Politicks of Great Britain and France," afford a body of unquestionable and conclusive evidence upon this point. It is much to be lamented, that after the publication of that incomparable work, any writer who lays claim to honesty and information, should dare to inculpate the allied powers for the guilt of the revolutionary war. Some of the above quotations from the speeches and writings of the revolutionary authors of the war were noticed by Mr. Marsh.

portions, and bore in his aspect the demonstrations of innate hopeless depravity, which plainly shewed " that he was come to bite the world." With no prœternatural spirit, it might have been foretold even at that hour

> "That many an old man's sigh, and many a widows,
> "And many an orphan's water-standing eye;
> "Men for their sons, wives for their husbands' fate,
> "And orphans for their parents' timeless death
> "Should rue the hour that ever he was born."

It is a right of nature to prevent the approach of danger by all measures of precaution. It is a natural duty and a fundamental principle of human justice, to prevent the triumph and repetition of great crimes by early vindictive visitation. If Ravillac or Damien, after the assassination of a king of France, or Ankerstroom after the murder of a King of Sweden, or the projector of the great treason against our protestant government in the reign of King James, had been detected lurking in some obscure corner, meditating without remorse upon his past atrocity, and sharpening a deadly weapon to perpetrate another crime of equal magnitude, who would censure as unjust or unnecessary, the disarming and punishment of that great offender, by any human authority? When the crime committed was the overthrow of the mightiest monarchy in Europe, and the massacre of its loyal supporters, upon a principle which naturally leads to the overthrow of all states, and the massacre of all sovereigns; and that crime was perpetrated by a huge association of merciless conspirators, exulting in their guilt, and making prodigious preparations to accomplish many more acts of similar atrocity, shall the rule of justice fail, because of the power and the number of the criminals? It would be vain to quote the publicists who have decided a question so simple and obvious; but it may be useful by way of illustration, to avail ourselves of an authority drawn from the Edinburgh Review, which has recently pronounced the war to be a manifest aggression on the part of the allies.

"The right of national interference (a late "refinement of this right of proportional im-"provement) has, like all other valuable and "sacred principles, been called in question. It "has been denied, that the total overthrow of "all regular government in the greatest nation "of Europe; the abolition of every salutary "restraint upon the operations of the multi-"tude; the erection of a standard to which "every thing rebellious and unprincipled might "repair; the open avowal of anarchy, atheism, "and oppression as a public creed:—it has been "denied, that the existence of this grand nui-"sance gave the vicinage (to use Mr. Burke's "apposite illustration,) a right to interfere. "Yet it is difficult to conceive what national "changes, except the introduction of the pes-"tilence, could give a better right to the "neighbourhood to reject all intercourse with "so infected a mass as France then was. And, "if such defensive measures were absolutely "necessary, it is evident, that the slightest ag-"gression on the part of this neighbour, justi-"fied that open war, which was so loudly pre-"scribed by the slightest chance of its leading "to a restoration of order. The immense ac-"quisition of power, which the French govern-"ment acquired by the Revolution; the gene-"ral levy and arming that immediately took "place, would have justified all neighbours in "extending their resources upon the common "principles of the modern system. Now, if

" this increase of French power had taken
" place on the Spanish, instead of the north
" side of the Pyrenees; if it had been not a
" sudden augmentation of internal resources,
" but an increase of territory and power by con-
" quest; no one doubts the propriety of an im-
" mediate interference; nay, if this increase had
" only been in contemplation, no one would
" hesitate to consider the formation of the plan,
" as sufficient cause for war; so thought our
" forefathers at least, when they attacked Louis
" XIV. a hundred years ago. But, what differ-
" ence is there, as to foreign states, whether
" such an augmentation of power takes place
" at the expence of the Spanish, the Bourbons,
" or at the least of the other branch of that
" illustrious house? Whether this sudden change
" in the aspect of one powerful rival neighbour
" is the consequence of her foreign conquests,
" or of her rapid internal changes? Whether
" the addition is drawn from the pillaged pro-
" vinces of Spain, or the overthrow of all the
" peaceful institutions, and the plunder of all
" the wealthy orders at home? When such a
" sudden and prodigious increase of resources
" takes place in one country, as can only be
" matched by a similar revolution, developing
" equal powers in the neighbouring nations,
" those neighbours are exactly in this dilemma;
" either they must wade through all manner
" of turbulence and danger, to the sudden pos-
" session of resources sufficient to balance this
" new power; or they must submit to this new
" power. One mode of escape only remains
" from alternatives equally cruel: they may unite
" against this common nuisance; they may in-
" terfere, and abate it. If France had con-

"quered the kingdoms of Leon and Castile, who
"doubts that Britain and Austria might have at-
"tacked her, though neither of them are friends
"of Spain? But this was not absolutely neces-
"sary; for, first, they might have perhaps saved
"themselves by defensive alliance, and the peace-
"able improvement of their internal resources;
"or secondly, they might certainly have ac-
"quired in Holland, or Denmark, or Spain it-
"self, an extent of territory, equal to that
"gained by France. But the former measure
"would have been dangerous; the latter both dan-
"gerous and unjust. In like manner Britain and
"Austria might have met the crisis of their af-
"fairs arising from the new and sudden acquisi-
"tion of resources which France made at the
"Revolution. First, they might have united de-
"fensively, as ancient allies, and worked all the
"while to improve their internal resources: or,
"secondly, they might have revolutionized, and
"followed the French example. The first, how-
"ever, of these plans would have been danger-
"ous; the latter both dangerous and unprin-
"cipled. One alternative remained; a union
"against the unheard of nuisance.

"We hesitate not, then, to lay it down as a
"principle, applicable to this extreme case, that
"whenever a sudden and great change takes place
"in the internal structure of a state, dangerous
"in a high degree to all neighbours, they
"have a right to attempt by hostile interference,
"the restoration of an order of things safe to
"themselves; or, at least to counterbalance, by
"active aggression the new force suddenly
"acquired. If a highwayman pulls out a pistol
"from his bosom, shall we wait till he loads
"and

" him? Shall we not attack him with like arms
" if he displays such weapons, whether he takes
" them from his own stores or seizes them
" from some other person in our sight? We
" do not attack a neighbouring nation for plun-
" dering or conquering a third power, because
" we wish to avenge or redress the injury, but
" because we shall be ourselves affected by its
" consequences. Shall we be less injured by
" the same consequences, because the dangerous
" power of doing us mischief, is developed from
" its recesses within, and not forcibly snatched
" from without?"

Never did the press send forth a more ample refutation of the principles recently advanced by the Edinburgh Reviewers, nor has the natural incurable guilt of the revolution been, at any time, more justly illustrated than in the preceding extract taken faithfully from an article upon Segur's work, ' Sur la Politique de tous les Cabi-
" nets" in the review published in January, 1802. At the time of that publication, the coalition of the princes of Europe was no recent occurrence, but all the causes and circumstances of that important transaction had been completely developed. Nothing has more recently transpired to blot that fair reputation of the grand alliance, and to cast a veil of purity over " the anarchy, atheism,
" and oppression" of the French Republic.

That war, which originated in the anarchy, atheism, and oppression of the French Republic, never ceased to rage, till the gigantic efforts of the revolution overcame all resistance, and established the throne of a mighty conqueror upon the ruins of the surrounding states. Are we now told that " France having been forced into
" those hostilities, and having been compelled

" to beat the allies from one end of Europe to
" the other, then took as little as she well could
" of their territory as a punishment for their past
" aggressions, and a security for their keeping
" the peace in future?" Never should we have imagined that the prodigious strides of the new tyranny made upon every side of its vast territory, breaking down every ancient barrier, and prevailing against all the efforts of confederated Europe, to limit its encroachments, would be characterized, at this day, as an instance of moderate ambition. Habituated to the principles of the system, which that tyranny has subverted, in which the weakest states were secure of their little territories, from the prevailing sense of justice, and the common interest by which the strongest were restrained; little did we expect even, that the first robbery of the Pope, by the seizure of Avignon, and the appropriation of the German territories, within the limits of France, made by the first national assembly, would have admitted such justification! But having seen that tyranny, growing to more insatiable injustice, sending forth ferocious armies on the territories of every neighbouring state, to advance like the torrent, which, with resistless impetuosity, sweeps away all the landmarks of ancient right, but never retires to its lawful channel: having witnessed the conquest and incorporation of the Netherlands, which were the bulwark of Europe, on that side, and of Savoy, which was the defence of Swisserland, and the rest of Italy; then looking to the subjugation of the United States, and to the devastation and plunder of the whole Italian peninsula; then remarking the overthrow of the Helvetic confederacy, that great monument of the

vigour and virtue of an heroic people in a distant age; then beholding the Emperor, while he still bore the sceptre of Charlemagne, brought to a disgraceful pacification, and yielding to triumphant regicide, the richest parts of his dominions, and the securities of what he was able to retain; afterwards observing the dissolution of the empire itself, and the parcelling of its impoverished states, among new created powers and principalities, subject to the will, and dependent upon the support of the haughty victor: when all this had been prescribed in treaty, and was confirmed as national law, by the desolating sword, and the treacherous counsels of an unexampled usurpation; when that usurpation had crushed all its enemies, and was flattered by the homage of all the powers of the continent, soliciting, at its footstool, a frail permission to retain the mere semblance of their glimmering independence; then observing that the thirst of dominion was yet unsatisfied, that the glories of the great Frederick must be extinguished, and Prussia undergo the common fate of servitude, which, by pusillanimous concession, she had vainly hoped to escape: In that aweful record of successful and overwhelming crimes; we cannot readily perceive one instance of that pacific temper, and "sufficient moderation," which France was "compelled" by the allies to abandon. Whatever were "the aggressions" of the allies, the vindictive wrath of their stern adversary seems to have felt little moral restraint. When we groan in sympathy with the palpitating victims, yet writhing under the scourge of their oppressor, which draws the life at every stroke, we neither acknowledge justice nor humanity, in that opinion, which considers such visitation as any spe-

cies " of punishment," for any past unproved
" aggression."

The war, on the part of this country, was equally inevitable. Soon after the fatal events of the tenth of August, the French legislature applied the principles of that insurrection to every monarchy in the world. On the 22d of that month, Dorat Cubiéres, in a discourse upon the eloquence of the French language, said to the Assembly, " Depuis que vous nous avez délivrés
" du mal des rois, de ce mal qui infecte encore
" la plupart des contrées de l'Europe, et dont
" j'espere que le genre humain sera bientot dé-
" livré a son tour, grace a vos sublimes décrets."
On the 4th September, the assembly took an oath; " Les representans du peuple jurent indi-
" viduellement haine aux rois, et a la royaute.
" Ils les combattront jusqu'a leur dernier sou-
" pir."

The convention, which soon after assembled, adopted all that republican ardour and universal hostility to kings. By their famous decree of the 19th November, they declared " que la na-
" tion Françoise accordera fraternité et secours
" à tous les peuples qui voudront recouvrer leur
" liberté; et le pouvoir executif est chargé de
" porter secours a ces peuples, et défendre les
" citoyens qui auroient été vexés ou qui pourroient
" l'etre pour la cause de la liberté." This decree was instantly followed by assurances of cooperation to the seditious societies of England, whose deputies appeared at the bar of the convention. On the 15th December, by another decree, it was declared " que la nation Françoise
" traitera comme ennemi le peuple qui refusant
" la liberté et l'egalité, ou y renonçant vondrait
" conserver, rappeller ou traiter avec le prince

" et les castes privilégiés." On the 19th December, Barailon observing that the English government had taken just offence at these obnoxious decrees, proposed, that they should be expressly restrained in their operation to those countries, " aux tyrans desquels la nation Fran-
" çoise sera enguerre." But the convention decreed " n'y avoir pas lieu a deliberer." "

The Journal Historique et Politique, a paper, at that time, considered as an authentic repository of the sentiments of the French government, on the 19th November, contained a consideration of the affairs of Ireland, which concludes with this remarkable passage. " Le peuple
" Anglois ne permettra pas sans doute à son gou-
" vernement de tenir l'Irlande, comme par le
" passé, dans le dépouillement des droits les
" plus sacrés des hommes et des peuples. Mais
" en supposant que ces deux isles sont ou se-
" ront bientôt déterminées a agir d'égale à égale,
" elles ont à traiter des questions bien interes-
" santes. 1°. Resteront elles sous une seule organi-
" sation sociale, où le canal St. George en feroit
" il deux peuples et deux souverains ? Dans le
" cas où l'union durera, continueront elles à
" avoir deux pouvoirs législatifs et un seul pou-
" voir exécutif, ou bien établiront elles l'unité en-
" tière de legislation comme d'execution ? Enfin
" continueront elles la Royunté ?

" On a beau faire; tous les contrats politiques
" des nations vont être renouvellés."

The same paper, on the 23d November, published the following article ; " Grande Bretagne.
" Point de Lords! Point de chambre haute!
" point de Roi! tel est le cri du peuple Anglois
" dans les rues de Londres, dans les rues des
" autres villes d'Angleterre ; tel est le cri qui ré-

" tentit dans les montagnes de l'Ecosse, et dans
" les plaines de l'Irlande. Puritains et Catho-
" liques leurs paroissent avoir ce meme dogme
" politique. Il n'y a que le roi d'Angleterre et
" peut-être quelques vieux Lords, honêtes gens,
" et quelques fripons de cour qui professent
" une autre religion sociale. Le parlement est
" prorogé jusqu'au mois de Janvier. Mais le
" mois de Janvier arrivera bientôt, et bientôt il
" faudra que George III. fasse un nouveau traité
" avec l'Angleterre qui lui donnera sûrement une
" bonne pension s'il se résigne à une révolution
" inévitable avec prudence." Let any candid mind, after noticing these extracts from the proceedings of the French legislature, and a government paper of France, decide whether or not the war was inevitable on the part of this country; and with what truth the Edinburgh Reviewers can say, that with us it was a manifest war of aggression?

The present circumstances of Europe impose upon us a duty more imperious and important than at any preceding period. If, by any means, Europe can be rescued from her present degrading subjection, to us are confided her hope and destiny. The patriots of Portugal and Spain, not declined in courage and resolution, nor appalled at the prospect of future difficulties, but yet loyal to their rightful sovereigns, look to us for liberal assistance. The King of Sweden, our ally, who in better times would have been regarded as the hero of Christendom, may yet repel misfortune, and demand our support. The Austrian Emperor, driven to renew that warfare from which he retired with the loss of dignity and dominion, and from which he can retire no more, even with a worthl hope to prosper in this his last effort, by the succour to be derived from our alliance. Contending in a common cause with us for the duties and the rights of all nations, he is entitled to expect it at our hands. The success of his efforts would inspire with new hope, the prostrate and desolated states which groan under the scourge of France, and after twenty years of unparalleled calamity, Europe might recover her freedom. It is only in that freedom that England can be securely and permanently great. Though France may not soon be able to wrest from us " our " ships, colonies, and commerce," which are the ultimate object of her policy, and for which she considers no price too great; and though in one series of events it will be our magnanimous resolution to defend that object in unextinguishable war, yet the fate of battle is precarious, and the acquisitions of victory are insecure, while contention lasts. Providence does not assure a triumphant result to any mortal undertaking:

—" Sua cuique exorsa laborem
" Fortunamque ferent: Rex Jupiter omnibus idem."

Our humanity sickens at the thought of unsuccessful or interminable war; our hope of renewed tranquillity, not less than our peculiar interest, animates us to co-operate with any sovereign opposed to France, if such co-operation increase the means of abating that gigantic power.

Great will be our guilt and folly after seventeen years of unrelenting opposition to revolutionary hostility, rewarded as they are with unabated prosperity and augmented potency, if we should now abandon that hope and interest, and sinking into the gulph of faction, should desert the government which has conducted us to greatness and glory, and should disappoint the hopes of Europe. This is not a time to parley about questions of abstract right, and to disunite the members of the state in matters of partial grievance. When the combined powers of all the orders should be exclusively devoted to combat an enemy which rejoices in our disunion, and would complete his triumph by promoting it, is it a less crime than that of political suicide to separate the people from their rulers, in action or affection, or to divert the public mind from hostility to France, by provoking its hostility to individuals at home; and by agitating questions of domestic policy, upon which we never can accord? Let us wait till Europe and ourselves are saved from the impending ruin, and till we can discuss domestic variances without gratifying the public enemy.

"Tum certare odiis, tum res rapuisse licebit;
" Nunc sinite, et placitum læti componite fœdus."

In the course of the last war, and of the present, none of the operations of our warfare have escaped the censure of disaffected writers. Their attempts have been unremitting to censure ministers for their plans; and frequently commanders, for the execution of those military enterprises, which were entrusted to their direction; while it was impossible that opinion could yet be founded on rational ground, or surmise be justified by evidence. The conspirators endeavour to root out of the public mind all confidence in the zeal and understanding of their rulers. Eminent success has been no shield against accusation. The triumph at Copenhagen projected and achieved, in a manner, which proved the energy and prudence of ministers, and added new glory to ou fallacious grounds of national justice, though no candid mind could doubt that the custody of the Danish fleet was necessary to prevent its falling into the hands of the common enemy, to be used by him for the invasion of this country. The Orders of Council made subsequently to similar regulations on the part of France, are condemned, though they are known to be the only means of checking a licentious neutral commerce, unjustifiable by the acknowledged law of nations, detrimental to the essential interests of our trade, and exclusively contributive to the resources of France. In just hostility they were introduced to shew to all the world that our rights, warranted by public law, cannot be violated with impunity, and that neutral nations, neglecting the duties, must forfeit the rights of neutrality; that acceding to the unjust pretensions of the enemy, they must participate in the punishment which we are able to inflict upon his temerity. The gallant conqueror at Vimiera was scandalized before it was possible to estimate the value of his services. Before any information had arrived to disclose the circumstances of the convention which closed that campaign, (by which, undoubtedly, "the hopes and expectations of "the country were disappointed,") an unprecedented clamour was excited, and punishment denounced without inquiry. To complain of public discussion in this country would betray ignorance of the constitution, and of the infinite value of the freedom of the press: but those public writers who, uniformly, with one voice, condemn all the measures of ministers, without the possibility of exercising a fair judgment; and labor to lower, in the estimation of the country, both the government and the legislature for defect of talent, and of, rectitude of intention, may justly be suspected of the worst design. They certainly may produce a most fatal result, at a time when all our united energies should be directed against that foe, whose triumphs, in other countries have been occasioned by the disunion of the people.

The measures pursued to break the vast combination of disaffected persons, which was organized in the affiliated societies, at the commencement of the last war, are stigmatized as " the English reign of terror."* Those societies were, at that time, established in perfect union throughout the empire for the avowed purpose of bringing about "radical reform," upon the principles then prevalent in France, and were in correspondence with the public enemy. The sagacious mind of Mr. Pitt detected that formidable conspiracy before it had acquired irresistible force, and, being armed with extraordinary power, his vigilance and vigour, at that aweful crisis, saved the monarchy, the legislature, and the laws. Let us not forget that he performed that difficult task without one capital conviction, without entrenching on the privileges of parliament, without dispensing with the trial by jury, and without the detention of one accused individual, except on suspicion founded on sufficient testimony. The constitution being saved, that extraordinary power was instantly surrendered, and the public liberties which, in practice, had never been violated, were perfectly restored. It is astonishing that a designation appropriate to that cruel tyranny which under the blood-thirsty Roberspierre had tortured mankind, should now be applied to characterize

* Edinburgh Review

those measures. It is impossible that those who love the British constitution, can denominate, "as the reign of terror," that period, when with the united voice of all loyal men, the government was impelled, by the necessities of an alarming peril, to assert the utmost majesty of the laws, and by the aid of parliament, was enabled, without the shedding of blood, to quell bold sedition, and repress traitorous conspiracy. When the Edinburgh Reviewers ostentatiously reprobate the proceedings of that day as "the English "reign of terror," they make themselves confederate with those who were then repressed, they oppose themselves to the principles then maintained by parliament, and avow the whole of their political system in its hugest deformity. With like asperity, the conduct of government in every department is now vilified and condemned. The wisdom and purity of parliament are disowned by a charge of corruption, venality, and weakness! The church, and its possessions are regarded with malignant jealousy, as the degrading appendage of an obsolete and expiring superstition, and an usurpation of men without utility or merit. The local magistrates, and the judges, whose uprightness might challenge investigation, are regarded with little reverence, and calumniated as the agents of oppressive laws. Without the possibility of truth, and in opposition to the statements of those who speak from authority and knowledge, the vulgar are persuaded that honor and promotion in the state, the army, and the navy, are not the reward of merit and the prize of service, but the acquirement of corruption, artifice, and intrigue. Opinion, which supersedes the powers of empire, and the institutions of antiquity, influenced by writers, who are popular because they are licentious, saps the foundations of established order, and threatens the superstructure of government.

But the most formidable engine of disaffection is the aspersion of character virulently applied to personages of exalted rank and illustrious station.

The profound wisdom of our subsisting institutions appeared in the separation of those classes, which are to exercise rule and magistracy, from the great mass of the community; that in their elevation of rank and superiority of function, the defects of personal character might be less apparent, and the imperfections of nature be lost in the splendour and dignity of factitious honour. It is not given to mortal power to purify the human heart by any political device from appetite, passion, and caprice, which near observers will always deplore in personages of the most exalted station. It is somewhere remarked, that no man is a philosopher in the eye of his own domestics. Such is our incurable frailty, that neither brilliancy of descent, magnificence of appointment, responsibility of trust, the influence of education, nor the possession of great and useful virtues, will eradicate from the mind many human qualities which cannot be exposed to common observation without exciting ridicule and contempt. The British constitution did every thing which human prudence could devise, by providing a veil of honour to be cast over that weakness and vice which inevitably exist in the highest characters, and by taking care that the purity of the laws should never be blemished in the hands of those who may be unhappily defiled by natural errors and offences.

It is important that we regard those whom the

law has made superior to us, with reverential awe. By levelling their moral qualities to the vulgar view, that object of our national policy is defeated. A learned writer * has insinuated, that the pious Massillon and the philosophic Fenelon may be classed among the conspirators against kingly government. In the Petit Carême, and in the Telemaque, which afforded useful lessons to the youthful princes for whom they were compiled, the wickedness and infamy of an oppressive, extravagant, and voluptuous reign, were forcibly and eloquently expressed. Their observations and recitals were pressed by corrupt writers upon the observation of a licentious age, and were applied, unhappily, to the monarchy of France. 'If Massillon and Fenelon, whose works were marked with sound religion and pure philanthropy, and were evidently intended to produce the most salutary effects, are justly chargeable with contributing to the greatest calamity that ever scourged the world, what judgment shall be passed on writers, whose daily employment and delight it is, to expose in shame and nakedness the foibles and the vices of illustrious persons, without, in any instance, commending their amiable qualities, or doing honour to their virtues.

He is indeed a parasite to power, and incapable of honorable sentiment, who considers wealth a privilege for transgression, or distinguished rank a cloak for immorality. The laws of England have not formed such a judgment; nor have they ordained one rule of conduct for the meaner classes, and another for the great and powerful. Our justice unsullied and severe, acknowledges

* Butler's Revolutions of the Germanic empire p. 200.

no distinction. But severe as is that justice towards those who shall be brought to its tribunal, it affords no sanction to the mean, unprincipled traducer, whose censure is intended not for punishment or moral reprobation, but for the political object of destroying all reverence and attachment of the lower classes towards the persons of authority and superior station. The moralist will always assert that equality of duty which exacts equal obedience from the monarch and the peasant. It is the office of the satirist peculiarly to chastise the licentiousness of the great, and to seek for the victims of his just reproach among the most elevated circles of polished life. But neither the moralist nor the satirist presumes to make his censure an instrument of political complaint; nor does he vilify the living character, or descend to personal abuse. The great Roman satirist, whose keen and manly exposure of the corruption of an abandoned age is a model to admire and imitate, was better acquainted with the nature of his duty.

" ——expenar, quid concedatur in illos
" Quorum Flaminia tegitur cinis, atque Latina."

Neither his example, nor that of any other, whose name may be ranked with the founders of sound and moral satire, will justify the fearless libeller, who exposes vice, not to chastise but to torture, and censures, not to improve but to destroy.

When in the reflections of the Weekly Register, and other disaffected pamphlets obtruded upon our notice, we observe an illustration and frequent recapitulation of the errors and vices of the great, paraded with an ostentatious display of sarcasm and ridicule; when they teach us to believe that the character of the higher classes is altogether licentious and corrupt; without one quality of goodness; we perceive that such reflections are dictated without justice or candour. When such men are indiscriminately scandalized, and the scandal terminates with an invitation to change, reform, and revolution, the motive of such calumny is obvious, and we detect the ultimate hope of the treacherous libeller.

If an honorable abhorrence of crime, and zeal for moral reformation occasioned complaint of that licentiousness, which in the present age pervades all classes, and from which the highest are not exempt, (always to be excepted from such concession is that pattern of goodness, who, notwithstanding the malignant insinuations of incorrigible slanderers, has long reigned in the love and veneration of his people :) however we may lament the natural tendency of such bold censure, yet we should regard it without personal indignation. But if the reviler selects, for his canting reprobation, those only to whom he is politically opposed, and can extol the virtues of such as belong to his own party, indifferent to their faults of similar quality and complexion, we may be sure that his motives are not pure, nor his censure liberal. In France at the commencement of the Revolution, the members of the royal house, and the whole order of the nobility, were reprobated for whatever laxity of manners their conduct disclosed, or malice could attach to their reputation; while the infamous Duke of Orleans, whose palace was the resort of persons blackened by all debasing and abominable crimes, was extolled for his justice and patriotism. In England, while the licentiousness of certain individuals is made a perpetual theme of rancourous condemnation, a late departed statesman, the leader of his party, (to whom allusion is made, rather than to the living, because the dead cannot suffer from reproach, and to whose many great and virtuous qualities, an impartial judgment is bound to render homage and admiration:) that able and eloquent advocate of the new maxims of philosophy is applauded for his fidelity to the public cause, and his unalterable love of liberty, with little notice of those immoralities, faults, and imperfections, which our generosity would forget or pardon, but which a rigid moralist must severely censure. While the personal transgressions of our higher classes are depicted in glaring colours, and with merciless precision, the atrocities which have accompanied the career of revolution pass without allusion; there are those who would excite our commonalty to insurrection, because a prince of the blood permitted his mistress to preside at a birth-day dinner, and because the lady, who was bound to another royal duke in illegal marriage, enjoys a pension from the crown;* (and it would be disgraceful to the country if she were without such provision.) With the sensibility of unsullied innocence, and with the rigour of stoical perfection, they detect and would slay the delinquent, however elevated, whom natural appetite has led beyond the limits of strict morality; but they express no apprehension of the fraud, intrigue, falsehood, outrage, murder, and oppression, inseparable from jacobinical revolution.

Appeal to the multitude upon questions which the law refers to a higher tribunal, and the publication of doubt and insinuation upon matters in which the lower classes are incompetent to form correct opinion, (and they are most prosperous and happy when their judgment is undisturbed by such bold casuistry,) whether made by the public enemy, or by the author of the Political Register, is equally pernicious. They can never be safely raised to the function of the national censor. The order of nature is by such means inverted. The subject is raised above his prince, and moral and political disorder must ensue. As the fluid will never ascend higher than its source, the judgment of the mob, in cases of that sort, will be low and abased, like the passion which suggests it; nor are they more able to dive for those merits which are deeply involved in perplexity and design. The substantial worth of the statesman sinks out of the fathom of their observation, while the shining tinsel of the shallow pretender floats on the surface to dazzle and betray them. At this time, to submit the vital principles of government, and the claims of the law, to the inquiry of such a judicature, is to destroy in the mind of the commonalty, the feelings of fidelity, respect, and love, necessary to our power and safety, and to prepare it for disastrous revolution and ignominious conquest.

The cold blooded calculator, who may fancy that he is raised above the generosities of our nature, who cannot sympathize with the affections of the heart, and who derives all his sense of duty from a comparison of advantage and compensation, may scoff at the moral feelings of mankind, and limit the social obligations by his sordid view of benefit and price. He may instruct the English nation that loyalty is a selfish principle, and patriotism an interested bias. In the language of Mr. Cobbett, he may state, "that loyalty is an empty sound,
" unconnected with the *general good*; that perso-
" nal friendship to a king forms no ingredient of
" loyalty; that the motive to resist Napoleon, and
" to make sacrifices for that purpose, will at last

"come to this; *to save ourselves from being in a worse situation than we are in under the family of Brunswick*; but that Napoleon could not carry the land to France, nor the goods; nor could he unstring the arms of a labourer, nor would it be his interest so to do."* He may also demand with the authority of adverse assertion, "*how*, in what manner a king can evince *paternal feelings* towards the country," and may point with cruel sarcastic question at the " age, infirmity, and illness" of a venerable sovereign.† He may traduce the active friends of government, as hireling, needy, and profligate antijacobins, the supporters of fraud and corruption from ignorance, imbecillity, or baseness; and he may represent our attachment to the state, and our terror of insurrection as " the foolish, the cowardly fear of *revolution*."‡

But such reflections are traitorous to that constitution, which we defend, not only for the sake of personal benefit, but jealously, with our lives and fortunes; they are incompatible with that duty which unites us to the prince by filial homage, as firmly as by strict obligation, and relaxes the sternness of power in the kinder affections of parental love; they are an abandonment of that patriotism which submits to all personal privation, rather than to national indignity; they are contrary to the example of our heroic ancestors, who at every period, sustained their sovereign as generously with the pledge of love as with the tribute of duty; who might have fallen, in his service, under the sword of an enemy, but could never speculate upon the *productive quality* of the soil, which con-

* Political Register, March 11, 1809.
† Political Register, March 25, 1809.

quest might not impair, or upon the *interest* which the victor would have in their future prosperity. Hopeless will be our condition when we shall balance that *interest* against the benignant protection which we have enjoyed, and yet enjoy under the family of Brunswick.

It is not probable that the British nation is deeply infected with that hostile spirit which labors to subvert the state. The revolutionary writers know that the people, collectively taken, are enthusiastically devoted to the constitution, zealously attached to the sovereign, and to his illustrious family, and conscious of the benefits they derive under the present establishments. By factious outcry, they may obtain the votes of municipal and provincial meetings, to censure ministers and statesmen, and to circulate the jargon of jacobinism in the form of public resolutions; yet they know that the authority of parliament still rests in the confidence and approbation of the weightier part of the country, which, upon any vital question, would give its voice, by vast majorities, in support of the legislature and the laws. They aim to make the people revolutionary upon questions subordinate and unimportant. By obtaining the censure of one member of the royal house, they think to cast disgrace upon the whole of it. By the approbation of a few active members of the lower house, (active only in opposition) they intend to pledge the nation in mistrust of the rest of parliament. By vehemence and loquaciousness in debate, the instant publication of their noisy eloquence, and an ostentatious enumeration of their numbers at assemblies, where the friends of government are hooted at, or dare not express their sentiments, they would appear to express the opinion of the great body of the people. While conspirators are active, it behoves the virtuous to be vigilant, lest their clamour, uncontradicted, may pass for truth, their voices unopposed have the force of unanimity, and their force unresisted obtain an easy conquest. As when the lion slumbers, he is easily entoiled in the hunter's net, as the citadel may be surprized by ruffians, if the garrison, however numerous, desert their posts, so may government, not upon its guard, be overturned in an instant, and the state be seized in contempt of its unsuspecting defenders. The nobles and the gentry are primarily bound to watch. Their rights and reputation are the first objects of attack, by those who have begun their hostility, in attempting by calumny and false aspersion to lower them in the estimation of the country.

We rarely meet with unmixed evil in the temper of mankind. If our virtues shine with diminished lustre, intermixed with error and infirmity, our vices are moderated and polished by honour, loyalty, and truth. Whatever faults may be attributed to individuals, among the illustrious families of England, they may boast of qualities which claim regard and admiration. In parliament, they are distinguished for their jealousy of the least violation of the public liberties, for their dutiful attachment to the laws, and their inflexible love of justice. In private life, they are not wanting in the duties of munificence, hospitality, dignity, and benevolence: while the censor may have ground for reprobation, the candid examiner will find more ample cause for generous commendation.

The offerings of thanks which are profusely tendered from the counties and corporations to Mr. Wardle, and the 125 members of his minority, public mind is already in a degree infected with that revolutionary principle which originates in contempt of constituted authority. With any principle of the British constitution they cannot be reconciled. At present the public can only err ignorantly, irritated by mistaken zeal, or misled by artful intrigue; but their measures may unhappily contribute to the triumph of desperate conspirators, who dare not as yet unfold their deep design. If the people, in public assemblies, may applaud in opposition to the sense of parliament, they may also censure. The hope of such applause, and the apprehension of such censure must influence the legislator's mind, which for every beneficial purpose ought to be entirely independent of that seductive recompence, and that formidable condemnation. Over the elected member of parliament, his constituents have no right to exercise direct controul, or to exert immediate influence. To judge his past conduct, to reward him with their continued trust, or to reject his future service with indignant displeasure, will be their function, when they shall be lawfully called to exercise the elective franchise. In parliament he is a representative of the whole nation, to be governed by no instruction from those who delegated him; it is his part to deliberate impartially for the commonweal of the undivided empire, and to decide honestly, unrestrained by the fear of the very few whose displeasure he ought not to dread; and not impelled by the hope of their favour, with which his duty is wholly unconnected. Such was the judgment of Mr. Burke, when he acted as the avowed advocate of the rights of the people; and upon that principle he was deputed to represent them by the popular party of the electors of Bristol; such will ever be the judgment of those who estimate the value of a supreme unawed national legislature.

The people have a right to influence the deliberations of parliament, by respectful petition, address, remonstrance, and complaint, and for such purposes they may meet in public assembly, consult, and determine. Their constitutional privilege extends no further. To extol a minority, to confer honour upon those whose counsel parliament has rejected, and to denunciate vengeance upon any one for his vote in parliament, whether that vote was ultimately sanctioned by the decision of a majority, or otherwise, or to question a determination of either house, to cast degrading censure upon its proceedings, and to express resentment against any member for the part which has belonged to him in such proceedings, is a violation of the independence of the individual member, a breach of the privileges of the legislature, an usurpation of a function which the law has not conferred, and an assumption of principle which tends to subvert the constitution, and to wrest the powers of deliberation and counsel from the authorities which now exercise them, to be vested, as in the tumultuous times of the revolution in France, in local conventions, municipalities, and self-constituted committees.

The Commune of Paris, which was an assembly of the electors of that department, claimed and exercised the right of instructing its deputies, of conferring civic honours upon those legislators whom they deemed patriotic, and of denouncing national vengeance upon such as were not in their judgment sufficiently revolutionary. They acquired a power far superior to that of the legislative body, and dictated its decisions. They became the main spring of the vast machine, which carried on the process of anarchy, slaughter, and devastation. May they be remembered by us as a fearful example!

The censure of Mr. Cobbett may be directed against these pages, as the work of a driveller, a minion adulator of rank, an enemy to freedom, or a shallow-pated courtier; " of a trading anti- " jacobin, or anti-every thing that is calculated " to draw the people together, and to afford " them a chance of communicating their ideas; " anti-every thing which does not tend to abso- " lute subjection."* Such an accusation and statement may captivate the vulgar ear, and create turbulent contempt of parliament, and of all those who are honest enough in these times to disregard a temporary popularity; and fearlessly to proclaim their sentiments of duty towards a meritorious government. Such may be the effect intended to be produced by the calumnies and aspersions of the Political Register. It were happy, indeed, if the scornful and unjust lash of that severity were only used to torture critically, or personally to traduce those who are yet bold enough to defend the principles of national order established by the British constitution. While it is extended to every member of the royal house, and to every personage of illustrious rank, to every legislator who supports the government, to every minister of the national church; to the sage and learned persons who administer and execute the laws in every tribunal of justice however dignified, to every servant of the state how-

* Political Register, 2;d April, 1809.

ever distinguished: while to bear the splenetic abuse of that licentious pen,

> "Is but the fate of place, and the rough brake
> "That virtue must go through."

it were mean to be silent in terror of the indiscriminate slanderer, or to retire in apprehension of his coarse illiberal satire.

It is frequently maintained by the friends of revolution, that the tranquillity of permanent government relaxes the character of mankind, and that genius languishes in the orderly ministration of affairs. The convulsions of states are alleged to produce heroic qualities, and to afford the means of advancement and exertion to whatever is most able and meritorious in the whole mass of society. There was never a statement more contrary to the truth of history; for although in the perplexity of changes, and in the tumult of civil discord, there have often appeared aspiring characters of prodigious capacity, who have raised themselves and their country far above the common level, yet the mental improvement of the world has been most conspicuous under different circumstances. After the termination of the religious wars, and the settlement of the balance of powers, a long period ensued in which all Europe enjoyed the security of regular government, and temperate orderly prosperity. During that period her advancement, in all science, martial and civil, her fertility of character and genius in every department, her acquisitions of successful experiment and discovery, and the universal prevalence of taste and literature in all countries, prove decisively that the tranquillity of lawful government is exceedingly propitious to the growth and cultivation of human intellect

Convulsive revolutions have rather a natural tendency to debase the human mind, and to check its progress towards improvement. The fathers of English poetry and the founders of the language had flourished under the patronage of the Plantagenets, before the civil wars occasioned by the doubtful title of the Lancastrian kings. The minstrels had already chaunted their melodies; Pierce Ploughman, Gower, Chaucer, and Lydgate, had perpetuated their harmonies in verse which we yet admire. The gloomy interval between the reigns of Henry V. and Henry VIII. does not furnish us with a single name, among the natives of England, deserving of much notice. Soon after, a period commenced when the lights of their own and future generations broke out in meridian splendor. In philosophy, divinity, natural science, poetry, and general literature, there arose a crowd of masters who yet preside in their several departments. There were More, Hooker, Jeremy Taylor, the translators of the Bible, the reforming fathers, Lord Verulam, eminent in all knowledge, Massinger, Spencer, Shakspeare, (in genius the mightiest among the mighty), Jonson, and their illustrious cotemporaries, whose fame has augmented in each succeeding age. Milton, if we do not refer his name to the same brilliant period, was yet the prodigy of an immediately succeeding day, and published his sublime productions to a revolutionary people, which had lost the judgment to discern, and the taste to relish the celestial harmony of his song.

Then came the puritanical and republican rebellion, to which the Edinburgh Reviewers, as reforming politicians, may attempt to reconcile us,*

* See their review of the life of Col. Hutchinson, Oct. 1808.

but on which, as critics and lovers of literature and science they cannot lavish their commendation. The savage violence of the factious parliament, the stern protectorate of Cromwell, and the gaudy but oppressive despotism of Charles, and James, all alike feverish and insecure, were unfavourable to the production or advancement of deep erudition and abstruse science; learning and taste seemed to languish under the controul of arbitrary power, or were strangled in the contentions of political parties.

At last came the glorious accession of King William, who having assured to us the blessings of sound government, rational religion, and general freedom, the mind delivered from the yoke of a restricted press, seemed to tower with energies unknown before, to the utmost height of intelligence and science.

Then arose a host of scholars, rational divines, deep philosophers, mathematicians, and poets, which afforded a lasting lustre to their time and country. There were Bentley, Boyle, Newton, Stillingfleet, and Locke, each supreme in his department. Then appeared Addison, Steele, Pope, Swift, Bolingbroke, and the writers who perfected the language, and justified the appellation of an Augustan age, attributed to that happy period. And this nation is yet illustrious in arts, literature, and science, as it is powerful in arms.

The monarchy of France, to the last moment of its downfal, was likewise renowned for liberal and profound knowledge, though its patronage was chiefly engrossed by wits and ostentatious theorists. The military despotism, which, in that country, has succeeded to popular faction, cannot be propitious to genius and literature. They will faint, and perhaps expire under the pressure of a savage tyranny, which dares not permit the interchange of opinions, or the free exercise of thought. Such is the natural and universal effect of revolution, and of the harsh malignant rule of an aspiring soldier, in which revolution naturally terminates. If we love the knowledge and mental pre-eminence which are at present our most amiable distinction, we shall dread the commencement of political discord, in which the brutality of ferocious ignorance may triumph over genius and learning, and when all the patronage of power will be engrossed by martial achievement.

Our wildest speculators, who complain of the oppression of the revenue, and the corruption and imbecillity of the public administration, wilfully obscure our vast national opulence growing with that revenue, and the power and political pre-eminence which are secured in that administration. While the capital becomes more splendid and enlarged; while other flourishing towns are created and extended; while a hardy population advances to fructify the soil, to convert the sterile deserts into fruitful plains, and to sustain the useful and ornamental arts; while the opulence of the higher classes, by a liberal expenditure, is devoted to encourage agriculture and commerce, and to reward the labor and ingenuity of the virtuous peasantry; while the seas, covered with a triumphant marine, sustain the riches of the whole earth floating to our shores, and bear the terrors of our prowess to appal our most distant enemies; in such prosperous circumstances, we may presume that the burthens of taxation are not generally oppressive, and that our governors are not altogether corrupt and unwise. Political science, though imperative as to our duties, yet as to questions of public right, is rather practical than speculative. The reform which will not augment the public prosperity and happiness, is not worth the blotted shreds of paper which are employed to recommend it. It behoves those who vilify and invalidate our establishments, to promise, as the price of revolution, a milder, more powerful, and happier system of government than that which they would subvert. They should entitle themselves to trust and support, not by fictitious imagery, but by assurance of real practical benefit. They should announce, as the reward of radical change, a greater magnificence of national institutions for public service and domestic accommodation; a more numerous and happier population; a more productive cultivation; more adventurous and prosperous manufactures; more ability of profusion to the higher, and more productive industry to the lower classes of society; a wider extent of advantageous and honorable traffic; and a prouder maritime dominion.

Publications evidently intended to produce revolution without any pretence of promising such results, the tendency of which must be injurious by endangering our present advantages, obtain currency among us by means of the freedom of the press. That privilege, the exclusive glory of our country, and the safeguard of our liberties, was the effect of King William's liberal government, which in 1693, permitted the restrictive statute of Charles the Second to expire.

It is the right of publishing our sentiments upon all sorts of subjects in free discussion, without restraint or previous licence, which creates the power of popular opinion terrible to tyrants, and, we trust, calculated to ensure the fabric of our constitution to the latest posterity. If that right were violated, there would be wanting a means of preventing those abuses which never can reach to a perilous height, while the public voice, with threatening authority, controuls the hand of innovation. Though great evils have resulted from the abuse of that right; though the measures of government, the wisdom of parliament, the independence of private reputation, and the particular interests of the community are often attacked by factious men, through the medium of the press; yet, as it is an essential branch of our constitution, and a sure preservation of the public liberties, there is no danger which will justify an abandonment of the important and invaluable franchise. Of all the rights which mankind enjoy, the freedom of the mind is that which ranks the highest. It is that which has imparted to the temper of our country its undaunted valour, its patriotism, and magnanimity.

While every one of noble mind, impressed with an ardent love of the public liberties, will tenaciously assert that freedom of the press, the palladium of England, he will nevertheless lament that the ministers of the laws have not always been sufficiently active in repressing its licentiousness. Works of impiety and immorality, false pretences for disaffection, and incitements to sedition have been published with boundless profusion. That evil may again recur; every good man will then call upon those who exercise authority to be vigilant and severe, not in restraining the freedom of publication, but in bringing to justice, and punishing those who, by such means, strike at the vitals of the commonwealth.

By the law of England, men are answerable for what they publish, and if it be an attack upon private character, or of dangerous tendency, they are obnoxious to legal penalty.

The Weekly Register, which has lately approached the utmost limit of free remark, compatible with public safety, complains of that restraint; and laments that the truth of libel should not be admissible in its defence in criminal prosecution. A member of parliament, on a late occasion, insinuated that the king's law officers were by no means slow to prosecute, nor the judges moderate to punish persons accused of libel. Those who have read the contemptuous and accusative aspersions recently cast upon the royal dignity, upon the highest personages in the state, and upon the public functionaries of all descriptions, and who witness the existing clamour for " change, radi-"cal reform, and revolution," may estimate upon what foundations are raised that opinion of Mr. Cobbett, and that suggestion of the honorable member.

As the imagination is more active than reason, and we often cast away a blessing which we possess, with the hope of obtaining something which fancy represents of higher value, it behoves us to be strictly on the watch, lest the advocates of jacobinism, assuming in this country the dialect and character of persons devoted to constitutional liberty, should enamour us of that guilty fiend which has betrayed so many nations to destruction. She will solicit our love with insidious smiles, and charm us with what resembles celestial harmony. But like another Circe, her sumptuous hospitality and envenomed cup will be the fraudful means to deprive us of all dignity and hope, to reconcile us to the husks on which we must ever after feed, and to level us with the embruted wretches already transformed by her accursed enchantment. Rather than yield to such seduction, let us trust to the antidote provided by the laws; if that should fail,

" Soon as she strikes her wand and gives the word,
" Draw forth and brandish our refulgent sword;
" And menace death; those menaces shall move
" Her altered mind to blandishment and love."

Critical and aweful are the times. Of all the nations which have been assailed by the treacherous artifice of the anti-social philosophy, England alone retains her liberty unimpaired, and her laws triumphant. She alone has fixed a barrier which the destroying angel cannot overleap, and has set a limit which he has not attempted to surpass. Faithful to the principles in which her safety has been found during a long and arduous contest, let her continue to defend her antient institutions, and to dread revolution. Let her children, like their gallant forefathers, declare to the whole world their attachment to their country and its laws, and to the presumptuous innovator, " unâ
" voce respondeant quod nolunt leges Angliæ mu-
" tare quæ usitatæ et approbatæ sunt." With fidelity to their sovereign and to their own honour, they may long defy their relentless enemy, and undismayed by the misfortunes of war, may at last prevail over his open hostility and the more formidable danger of domestic sedition. Remote posterity may attribute to them a glory greater than that of saving themselves and society from the political degradation which threatens the whole civilized world. It may be their peculiar honour, even yet, to rescue government, reason, and religion from the consuming gulph of false and cruel philosophy. It may be their lasting triumph, more to be desired than

" The spoils of nations and the pomp of wars,"

by the exercise of manly sense, the maintenance of lawful authority, the force of rational and reli-

E E

gious truth irresistible where it is applied, and the spirit of patriotism ennobled by an union with that of loyalty and valour, even yet to crush the conspiracy of that restless, rebellious, impious, and antisocial crew; (much to be dreaded in arms, but most when they creep and whisper with fawning flattery, and smile with unwrinkled brow in semblance of philanthropy)

"Qui ratione suâ disturbent mænia mundi
"Præclarumque velint cœli restinguere Solem,
"Immortalia mortali sermone notantes."

THE END.

ERRATA.

Page 8, Line 29, *for* second *read* inferior.
—— 20, —— 8, *for* uncapable *read* incapable
—— 35, —— 4, *after* combined *insert* with
—— 47, Note, *for* vellera *read* vellere, and insert a comma
—— 48, Line 12, *for* bareforked *read* bare, forked,
—— 65, Note, *for* Dauphin's *read* Dauphin
—— 73, Line 16, *for* Asistides *read* Aristides
—— 74, —— 31, *for* pretences *read* pretensions
—— 75, —— 3, *for* jacobin *read* jacobinical
—— 86, —— 25, *for* unanneal'd *read* unannell'd
—— 104, —— 16, *after* infidelity *insert* on the other
—— 105, —— 29, *for* country *read* community
—— 107, —— 7, *for* mutari *read* mutare
—— 109, —— 24, *for* unimpregnable *read* impregnable
—— 111, —— 20, *for* might *read* may
—— 145, Note, *for* Baurel *read* Baruel
—— 146, Line 14, *for* to exclaim *read* in exclaiming
—— 151, —— 5 from the bottom, *for* be *read* were
—— 152, —— 28, *for* though *read* thought
—— —— —— 29, *for* corresponding *read* correspond
—— 172, Note, *for* deserant *read* deferant
—— —— —— *for* contens *read* contents
—— 183, Line 29, *for* Royunte *read* Royaute.

Lately Published by the same Author,

REFLECTIONS
ON
SOME QUESTIONS RELATIVE
TO THE
PRESENT STATE
OF THE
NATION,
IN A
LETTER
TO THE
Rev. Dr. RANDOLPH.

"What damned error but some sober brow
"Shall bless it, and approve it with a text,
"Hiding the grossness with fair ornament."